# A Galaxy of Games and Activities for the Kindergarten

**Also by the Author:**

*Individualized Techniques and Activities
for Teaching Slow Learners*

# A GALAXY OF GAMES AND ACTIVITIES FOR THE KINDERGARTEN

Joyce Lewallen

**Illustrations by: Delphine Minor**

PARKER PUBLISHING COMPANY, INC.  West Nyack, New York

© 1978, *by*

PARKER PUBLISHING COMPANY, INC.

West Nyack, N.Y.


*All rights reserved. No part of this*
*book may be reproduced in any form or*
*by any means, without permission in*
*writing from the publisher.*

Library of Congress Cataloging in Publication Data

Lewallen, Joyce.
   A galaxy of games and activities for the kindergarten.

   Includes index.
   1.  Kindergarten--Methods and manuals.  2.  Creative
activities and seat work.  I.  Title.
LB1169.L49       372.21'8               78-17171
ISBN 0-13-346106-8

Printed in the United States of America

*In loving memory of*
*my mother*

**Dorothy Dyer Neal**
**April 26, 1904 to August 1, 1977**

*and*

*my father*

**James Perry Neal**
**November 29, 1898 to October 10, 1971**

# How This Book Offers the Kindergarten Teacher Simple and Effective Ways to Develop Necessary Skills

This book is written for the "busiest of all busy teachers" —the kindergarten teacher. It gives you a complete activity and game reference book covering every aspect of a kindergarten curriculum. Among others, you will be able to choose an activity quickly and easily to teach a skill, to reinforce a concept, to build a background for future skills, or perhaps, to test a skill. For instance, you will want to discover which children can recognize their name and can put the letters in sequential order. With one of the games prescribed for this, each child chooses other children, who hold the letters of his name, and arranges them in the correct order. If he repeatedly reverses the order, you immediately find a child with a perceptual problem, or perhaps, this child sees only the tall letters, or he chooses the wrong letters altogether. You have valid test results obtained through an enjoyable game.

The ideas generated in this book are based on the premise that coordination development is essential before a child can achieve at his highest ability level. In the kindergarten galaxy, coordination development, both large and small, can be viewed as a representation of the sun in our solar system. Since coordination is essential to the complete and full development of every child, it is the focal point of kindergarten education. Planets are represented by the subject matter that revolves around, and obtains strength from, coordination, or the sun. The moons and satellites which revolve around the planets and obtain their light

7

source from the galaxy core—our sun—are symbolized by the different types of activities through which we teach coordination while developing subject matter skills. Other satellites are illustrations of sensory receptivity and social and emotional adjustment.

Each phase of the child's early childhood depends upon the sequential development of coordination skills. Then, as with the sun, these skills reflect their strength through special activities which in turn are mirrored in the child's ability to perceive new concepts. These new concepts then are reflected outward in the basic skills.

We begin this large and small coordination development in the first chapter. All of the activities are simple, yet effective in producing coordinated children capable of performing the fine motor requirements of future school years. For instance, a simple game of ball requiring the children to use only their feet to maneuver the ball from one team to another is indicative of the type of activity included in the first chapter.

Because kindergarten teachers are always in need of new and exciting art activities, many simple and delightful projects are not only included in the chapter on art, but throughout the book. You will find that many of these art projects teach very basic skills. Since art is one of the most intriguing and thought-provoking avenues open to you, many activities that strengthen eye-hand coordination, which is essential for future reading and writing experiences, are incorporated in nearly every chapter. One example of this type of activity is stringing small pieces of straws and buttons or colored paper cut in shapes to represent monthly holidays, such as hearts, bells, pumpkins, shamrocks, and so on. They make lovely borders for bulletin boards or they can be used for other room decorations—so pretty, yet so simple and easy.

How exciting it is to take the musical activities throughout the book and teach basic skills and coordination development! You will find them as delightful as the children. It is fascinating to watch kindergarteners learn their colors while enjoying the exercises performed to Hap Palmer's recording, "Colors." For developing math skills, you will be as enthusiastic as I was when I first used Henry Glass's and Rosemary Hallum's recording, "Monsters," or Hap Palmer's "Marching Around the Number Wheel." The selections "Stop, Look and Listen" and "Brush Away" contribute to a fascinating and positive approach to health and safety. Or perhaps you wish to record your own music, or you would like to use recorded music without words. Whatever your desire, you will be able to reach your goal through the activities provided here.

Through such avenues as art, music, and coordination exercises, you will find that intriguing and exciting scientific concepts are being developed. For example, is it a science lesson or coordination development that you wish to project? You will be teaching both as children gather different kinds of fall leaves to make a leaf family or Halloween characters as an art project. Can you not see an old bat flying around with its two leaf wings? Or, the witch riding her broom, which is really willow leaves?

In kindergarten, we are concerned with helping children feel emotionally secure in an ever-expanding environment. And as we guide our children to an awareness of other races and cultures, acceptance of others as not unlike ourselves becomes one of our prime objectives.

Through activities that provide children with useful information about themselves, a separate and important societal entity is taking shape in each child's mind. As our activities spread outward, this same group of children learns that another child in a far-away land is experiencing the same joys, fears, apprehensions, and needs as they are. Our job is complete when we instill in children the acceptance of self and others as equal human beings.

Because you are responsible for implementing correct writing procedures, enough activities are included or suggested in the fourth chapter and elsewhere in the book to cover the subject from the stages of pre-writing to paper and pencil exercises. You will find sequential activities to teach both letters and numerals as the children engage in coordination exercises, art, and music.

Five-year-olds must have the opportunity to change activities frequently, but these activities must also correlate with the goals and objectives of the content areas. While the games and activities in this book are simple, they are uniquely designed to be effective in teaching the pre-skills that children will need when they leave kindergarten. Whether you need an activity to develop visual, auditory, and tactile perception to ensure correct symbol-writing habits, or to develop pre-reading and math skills, these choices, and many others, are here for you to use.

The materials needed, the objectives, and the skills that each activity develops are given with each activity in order to better facilitate your task of developing and preparing daily lessons. They offer you, the busy teacher, immediate skill-producers with little preparation time. A few records, art materials, rhythm instruments, gym equipment, and odds and ends, all readily available, are all that is required.

The involvement of the children in active participation provides the stimulus necessary for exciting and exhilarating learning situations. These situations cover the gamut of a well-rounded kindergarten program. Yet, they are easily and readily adaptable to *any* classroom with minimum preparation time.


**Joyce Lewallen**

# Acknowledgments

I am indebted to Donna Swanson, who spent much of her time reading the manuscript, giving suggestions, and making helpful contributions. As expert kindergarten teachers, Donna and Sheryl Seaman gave invaluable supplemental recommendations for improving upon my ideas.

To Marilyn Peden I owe sincere appreciation for the music she provided for one of my songs. And, as with my last book, I am grateful to Delphine Minor for her diligence in providing the artwork. Through her able assistance, many activities were provided with illustrations that clarified what I could not put into words.

# Contents

Coordination Development: The Basis on Which to
Build a Successful Kindergarten Program . . . The
First Ten Weeks of School: Increasing Proficiency of
the Larger Muscles with No Equipment . . . Effec-
tive, Stimulating Experiences with Minimum
Equipment Requirements . . . Activities Involving
The Balance Beam . . . Developing Dexterity
Through Ball Use . . . Bustling Group Executions
. . . Effective Bean Bag Maneuvers . . . Having Fun
with Jump Ropes and Hula Hoops . . . Shaping Fine
Motor Control Through Ordinary Kindergarten
Materials . . . Cultivating Eye-Hand Coordination
with Hand-Made Materials.

Why Music Is the Universal Language . . . Enjoy Music and Games As You Develop Coordination . . . How to Produce Musical Selections to Accommodate Your Special Needs . . . The Aesthetic Enjoyment Gained Through Combinations of Art and Music . . . Using Recordings to Foster Exciting Learning Experiences . . . Examples of Activities That Can be Derived from Recorded Music . . . Using Music to Encourage Correct Numeral and Letter Writing.

The Immeasurable Realm of Art in Kindergarten . . . Incorporating Simple Shapes in Art Activities . . . Using Nature's Abundance to Amplify Science Studies . . . Creating with Ordinary School Supplies.

Key Roles Games Play in the Kindergarten Program . . . Games and Activities Adaptable to Classroom and Party Use . . . Favorite Games That Develop Coordination . . . Developing Skills Through Races . . . Relays That Add Excitement to Learning.

Why Science is Important in the Kindergarten Curriculum . . . Techniques That Contribute to Scientific Language Skills While Learning About Autumn . . . On the Inside Looking Out at the Wintry Conditions . . . How to Have Fun in the Spring with Science Activities . . . Using the Calendar to Learn About Spring.

# 1

# Assuring Successful Kindergarten Experiences Through Coordination Development

## Coordination Development: The Basis on Which to Build a Successful Kindergarten Program

The most wonderful experience you can offer your students when they enter the kindergarten universe is a program of large motor coordination activities slowly integrated with small motor experiences. Couple these with language development, along with the background information and basic skills they'll need when introduced to the first grade, and you have the basis for a kindergarten curriculum that cannot fail.

When students understand the language used in instructions, they can perform properly. Therefore, it is assumed that all language used in giving instructions has been previously learned or is clearly defined.

Add your own ideas to the following suggestions and you

should have a world of activities that will not only be exciting to your children but also to yourself.

## The First Ten Weeks of School: Increasing Proficiency of the Larger Muscles with No Equipment

The following activities contain only a minimum of suggestions. You should add many others as you progress through them. Make a card file with a card for each day of the year, changing and adding to it as you see the need. Begin the first day of school and continue throughout the school year. Never be in a hurry to get to the next level. Children must succeed every day for these activities to be fun and for them to achieve the desired objectives.

*Objectives for the first ten weeks of school:*

1. To begin the large motor coordination activities involving the large muscles of the legs, feet, arms, and hands.
2. To develop an understanding of the language skills necessary to satisfactorily complete assigned activities.
3. To learn specific working areas and the rules for participating in the activities.
4. To develop listening and concentration skills.
5. To encourage self-discipline.
6. To ensure successful experiences.
7. To increase sensory receptivity.

### First Week of School: "Boundaries and Rules"

*Procedure:*

Assign a large area and explain the boundaries to the children. If you have a gym, half of it is perfect. Assign each child a home base within these boundaries that gives him or her freedom to move without touching anyone. A home base is a spot assigned to each child to which he always returns following an activity and he always begins each day. Hula hoops make good markers for bases, or blocks with names written on them are beneficial at first. These help children to learn their names early in the year. For more information concerning home bases and for activities suitable for kindergarteners, refer to my previous book.*

Tell the children that they are not to touch another child during activities unless it is unavoidable. This is a coordination exercise within itself, and it forces each child to perform independently of another.

During the first week, your time should be spent in teaching each child his home base, starting and stopping to a whistle, what "freeze" means, and how to follow specific instructions. They should be taught to stop immediately, or "freeze," when they hear the whistle, and should not start an activity until you sound the whistle, even though you may have given the directions. Take as long as necessary each day to show each child where he is to stand, as this will save more time than any other factor.

Any activity this week should be confined to walking within the specified area. If time permits after finding the base each day, the following activities may be practiced:

1. Walk forward in a straight line, (Blow the whistle to start. After a few seconds blow the whistle to "freeze.") Walk back to home base. (Blow the whistle to start. Hereafter, blowing the whistle will not be mentioned, but use it before and after each activity.)

2. Walk around in a big circle. Walk in a small circle. Walk back to home base.

3. Walk around a friend. Walk with a friend without touching him. Walk back to home base.

4. Any similar walking activities. Be sure to write all activities on a card for future use.

---

*Joyce Lewallen, *Individualized Techniques and Activities for Teaching Slow Learners* (West Nyack, N.Y.: Parker Publishing Co., Inc. 1976), Chapter 1.

## Second Week: "Walk and Run"

*Procedure:*

Still using the same area as last week, have the children perform variations of the walking and running theme. For instance:

1. Brisk walk; slow walk.
2. Slow run; fast run.
3. Slow walk; slow run.
4. Fast run; slow walk.
5. Combinations you choose.

## Third Week: "Hop and Tiptoe"

*Procedure:*

Add variations of the walking and running theme, then add
hopping on both feet and tiptoeing. Use short distances for hopping. Some suggestions are:

1. Walk as an elephant; hop as a rabbit.
2. Walk briskly; hop slowly; run as a mouse.
3. Hop slowly; tiptoe slowly; hop as a bird.
4. Tiptoe briskly; walk slowly; run quickly.
5. Add other animal and vehicle movements.

## Fourth Week: "Leap and Jump"

*Procedure:*

1. Take giant steps; go back to home base using baby steps.
2. Walk backwards; jump forward.
3. Run slowly; run faster; faster; slowly; walk. (Each command is new. Start and stop each with the whistle.)
4. Leap high; jump low.
5. Run with arms straight out; walk with arms overhead.

## Fifth Week: "Slide"

*Procedure:*

1. Slide forward; hop backward.
2. Jump forward two times; slide backward.
3. Pretend you are a jet taking off; now you are flying; now you are coming in for a landing.
4. Hop to one side; hop to the other side.
5. Slide to one side; slide to the other.

## Sixth Week: "March and Gallop"

*Procedure:*

1. March as a soldier; gallop as a horse.
2. Gallop forward; slide backward.
3. Gallop in a circle; turn around and march back.
4. Slide in a circle, stopping where you started.
5. Leap as a kangaroo; waddle as a duck; add others.

## Seventh Week: "Skip and Hop"

*Procedure:*

Add hopping on one foot and skipping. These are hard for children. Although hopping can be done, start with three hops and progress to ten throughout the year. Teach children to skip by saying, "Step, hop." (Pause.) "Step, hop." Older children can often help better than a teacher. Assign an older child to each kindergartener who needs to learn to skip. Let the ones who can skip perform within the regular area. Some activities may be:

1. Hop on one foot three times forward; turn around and hop on the other foot to home base.
2. Skip forward; turn around and skip back.

3. Hop on one foot around home base; hop on the other foot around the base.

4. Skip around the base; skip around several bases.

5. Skip forward; walk backward: add others.

## Eighth Week: "Evaluation"

*Procedure:*

Use this week for testing. Use a parent, aide, or older students to work with the other children while you test five or six students at a time. Make a check list on a master set and mark those activities the children can do, they cannot do, and those on which they need further practice. Your check list may look something like Figure 1-1. As you go through the year, you will need to make other check lists. You may add specific actions if you wish, such as the fourth example, but some teachers may not wish to be this explicit. Make dividing lines between items and vertical lines for check-mark areas.

## Ninth Week: "Review"

*Procedure:*

Continue with any activities on which children need more work. This will definitely include skipping and hopping on one foot. All of the preceding activities should be continued throughout the year, but you should continually add more complex and varied maneuvers. Add many animals, tools, equipment, and vehicles.

## Tenth Week: "Variations"

*Procedure:*

1. Skip with one arm up and one down; skip while the body is held high (on tiptoes, arms outstretched); skip while it is low (squatting or any way the child wishes to lower the body).

| Name: | Achievement | | |
|---|---|---|---|
| | yes | no | needs improvement |

1. Follows directions
2. Knows home base.
3. Freezes on command.
4. Walks forward.
   backward.
   to either side.
   fast; slow.
   as specific animals.
5. Runs. (Add specific actions
   if you wish.)
6. Hops on both feet.
7. Tiptoes.
8. Jumps or leaps on both feet.
9. Slides.
10. Marches.
11. Gallops.
12. Hops on one foot at least
   three times.
13. Skips.

**Figure 1-1**

2. Run with hands clasped behind the back.

3. Pretend to be walking a tightrope, balancing with the arms outstretched.

4. Walk angrily; sadly; happily; against the wind; hurriedly; in a snowstorm; etc.

5. Pretend you are climbing a steep mountain; now you are coming down; you are on level ground; now you rest.

### Effective, Stimulating Experiences with Minimum Equipment Requirements

The only equipment that you actually need is described in this chapter. You may have some other equipment to use, and if so, you can develop some similar activities for its use. The equipment required is minimal, but it should be a part of every kindergarten room. The following suggestions for equipment activities cannot even begin to cover a full year. Continue throughout the year, adding more difficult experiences as the children advance in coordination.

*Objectives for activities using equipment:*

The objectives for non-equipment activities are also applicable to activities with equipment. Others that can be added are:

1. To increase coordination for handling equipment of all sizes and shapes.
2. To increase coordination of eye-hand and eye-foot movements.
3. To ensure increased success, and thus the pleasure, of the children.
4. To increase the vocabulary. (This objective applies to any kindergarten activity, and it should not be minimized.)

## Activities Involving the Balance Beam

#### #1. "Line Walking"

*Procedure:*

In preparation for walking balance beams, you should spend a few days letting the children walk on all kinds of lines. These are only a few suggestions:

1. Playground areas marked for four-square, hopscotch, dodgeball, etc.
2. Cracks in the paved areas; sidewalk edges, if available.
3. Any marked areas in the room such as: carpet edges, tile lines, taped strips, etc.

#2. "Flat Beam"

*Procedure:*

To start on the balance beam, first lay it flat on the floor, wide side up. Let the children achieve success at walking across this before they are required to walk the beam in its stands. Some will be ready before others. The narrow side of the beam should not be used until late in the year.

Children should have rubber soles on their shoes, wear tennis shoes, or take off both shoes and socks. Socks and slick soles are very dangerous. Have a mirror at one end of the beam so the children can see their feet in it as they walk rather than to look down at them. The mirror need not be expensive. A nine-by twelve-inch one in a frame set against some object is fine. Or, if you prefer a larger one, one of the long ones in a frame to be put on a wall has a better mirror than those in the stands.

#3. "Forward Walk"

*Procedure:*

After the beam is put in the stands, allow each child sufficient time to become proficient at walking forward before you add complex activities. Walking forward is done in two ways. The easier method is to walk across as if you were walking across the floor. The harder way is to walk heel-to-toe across the beam. Master these two activities before trying other maneuvers.

#4. "Changing Positions"

*Procedure:*

1. Walk to the middle, turn around, and walk back.
2. Walk to the middle, walk backward to the end.
3. Walk to the end, walk backward to the other end.

4. Walk backward to the end, walk forward to the other end.

5. Walk sideways across the beam.

6. Slide forward across beam, slide backward to the other end.

7. Slide sideways across beam, walk backward to the other end.

8. Add other executions as the children progress.

## #5. "Acrobatics"

*Procedure:*

1. Walk across the beam while bouncing a ball to the side.

2. Walk across while balancing a beanbag on the head; then on the back of the hands; then on the shoulders; add different positions and types of walking while balancing beanbags.

3. Throw a ball to someone while walking across the beam.

4. Count to ten, say a rhyme, sing a short song, etc., while walking forward.

5. March as a wooden soldier; take baby steps; take giant steps; balance two balls in hands held straight out from the body.

6. Add numerous other acrobatic activities.

## Developing Dexterity Through Ball Use

## #6. "One-Child Fun"

*Procedure:*

Each child should have access to a nine-inch ball for use throughout the year. Large balls are used more for group activities and for free-time play. Foam balls are used for dodge ball or some ball games played inside.

1. Bounce the ball one time and catch it.
2. Bounce a specified number of times.
3. Bounce on an accented musical beat.
4. Bounce as many times as teacher claps. (Turn your back to the class when you clap.)
5. Bounce and clap before catching the ball.
6. Bounce the ball while in a squatting position; bounce while tiptoeing; bounce while skipping; etc.
7. Alternate hands while bouncing the ball.
8. Bounce without looking at the ball.
9. Move around home bases bouncing a ball without running into friends.
10. Throw the ball up, move under it, and catch it before it bounces; throw it up, turn around, and catch it before it bounces.

## #7. "Partner Work-Out"

*Procedure:*

1. With your partner, sit down and roll the ball to each other.
2. Throw the ball underhanded to your partner, catch on return. Do the same overhanded.
3. Bunt the ball with one foot from one partner to another.
4. With a ball for each partner, see who can dribble the longest, the highest, the lowest; while squatting, sitting, skipping, etc.
5. Throw the ball to a partner, who must turn around and catch it before it bounces; add other activities.

## Bustling Group Executions

Before performing group activities, you will need to give instructions as to what is to be done and what is not to be done, or these activities could get out of hand. More group games using balls will be found in Chapters 6 and 8.

## #8. "Foot Bunt"

*Procedure:*

Divide your class into two groups with a dividing line drawn between them. Boundary lines are also drawn around all sides. The object is for each side to bunt the ball with their feet only, no hands, to the other side. If either team allows the ball to go outside the outer lines on their side, they lose a point. The team with the most points wins. This could also be played with smaller groups, and you will have greater success doing so.

## #9. "Hand Bunt"

*Procedure:*

Using the same boundary lines, the teams are to bunt the ball with their hands to the next team without it touching the floor or ground. If the ball touches the ground or goes outside the boundaries on either side, that side loses a point. This game should be played during the latter part of the year.

## #10. "Keep Away"

*Procedure:*

Form teams of six or eight students. Using a large circle or square for a boundary, with a line drawn in the center, half of each team is on each side of the center line. If the ball moves across the center line, the members of a team on that side try to keep it from the other team, and vice versa. Team members may not cross the center line. When the ball goes out of bounds, the team responsible for the loss loses a point. Some activities that can be used in Keep Away are:

1. Bunting with the feet from one member to another.

2. Bunting with the hand without the ball touching the floor.

3. Bouncing once between members.

4. Throwing to team members without letting the ball bounce.

5. Bunting with either the hands *or* the feet.

These games require some degree of coordination and should either be reserved until the end of the year or for especially well-coordinated children.

## Effective Beanbag Maneuvers

Not only can beanbags be used individually as well as in groups, but they can be used as balancing objects in other activities. They can also be used in games. Some simple beanbag maneuvers follow. Add to these as the children advance through the year.

### #11. "Beanbag Solitaire"

*Procedure:*

Each child has his own beanbag for these activities. You can either make or purchase beanbags, but each child should have one.

1. Toss up, catch with one hand; catch with two hands.

2. Toss up with one hand, catch with the other.

3. Toss rapidly from one hand to another; try this later with eyes closed.

4. Toss up, catch at your side; catch at the back.

5. Toss up and slightly out, run under it and catch it before it touches the floor.

6. Toss forward a short distance, run and catch it before it touches the floor.

#12. "Beanbag Sharing"

*Procedure:*

1. With a partner, throw to each other and catch on return.
2. Throw to a partner who turns around before catching it.
3. Clap three times after beanbag has left the partner's hands.
4. With several other team members, try to keep the bag away from the opposing team.
5. Try to toss the bag into a container. Use large containers at the beginning of the school year, but progressively use smaller ones.
6. Toss through holes in a figure. These can either be made out of cardboard or bought. Clown figures make good ones with the holes placed where the dots on the costume should be.
7. Add increasingly difficult maneuvers.

## Having Fun with Jump Ropes and Hula Hoops

#13. "Jump Ropes"

*Procedure:*

If children learn to jump rope in kindergarten, that is sufficient. Some girls do very well, while boys, either because they think it is "sissy" or because of disinterest, usually have a very difficult time learning. Teach them, encourage them, and, if at all possible, have an athlete who trains with the rope talk with the boys and show them the maneuvers he does with the rope. Older students should be engaged to help teach the little ones how to jump, as you need to have a one-to-one situation. Every child should have a rope. Buy long pieces of rope and have them cut to size, tying them off at the ends. They are much stronger and cheaper. Buy enough to have a couple of longer ropes since group jumping is prevalent in the springtime. You might even challenge another kindergarten class to a contest.

#### #14. "Hula Hoops"

*Procedure:*

Each child should have access to a hula hoop. It is a good coordination builder and it is fun. Children like to try all kinds of tricks while twirling the hoop around their waists. Some of the activities they might try while twirling are:

1. Twirling smaller hoops around wrists or ankles. The size used for ring toss is good for this.
2. Walking, running, skipping, hopping, squatting, etc.
3. Keeping time to music through clapping, tapping, performing actions, etc.
4. Walking a line. Some can do it on the balance beam, but be careful who tries this on the beam.
5. Add others.

## Shaping Fine Motor Control Through Ordinary Kindergarten Materials

Eye-hand coordination is absolutely essential if children are to do well in basic skills. No child can do justice to subject matter until he has perfect control over his hand and eye movements. The best sources from which to choose activities are art projects. However, there are many materials found in most kindergarten rooms just waiting to be used as coordination-developing kits. Maybe you are not aware that the following materials are actually coordination promoters. The only requirement is to see that each child carries through with any task he starts. If it is obviously too difficult for him, a similar type of less difficult material should be given to him.

1. Puzzles.

2. Templates. (Stencils.)

3. All types of blocks.

4. All building materials such as Lego℗ sets, Lincoln Logs,℗ Tinker Toys,℗ and so on.

5. One-inch square blocks, pegboards, and beads for stringing—all of which come with sets of pattern cards—a must for kindergarten. (Also see Chapter 4.)

6. Any other material found in your room. Develop objectives and special lessons from which children can gain fine motor contol.

7. You are reminded to continue making note cards of all daily activities.

*Objectives of classroom materials:*

1. To develop small muscular coordination.

2. To increase language development.

3. To increase capabilities for increasingly difficult assignments.

4. To develop persistence and self-control.

5. To increase enjoyment of available materials.

6. To increase perception for shape, color, and size.

7. To develop thought processes and ingenuity.

## Cultivating Eye-Hand Coordination with Hand-Made Materials

### #15. "Follow Along"

*Procedure:*

To develop that fine motor control needed for writing and reading, you can spend a hundred dollars or more, or you can make your own very easily. All you need are master sets and imagination. The students need a crayon and concentration. You have seen them on the market—two lines drawn for children to trace between. The following are only suggestions. Tell the children that they are to pretend their crayon (never use a pencil) is a car, and if it wavers from the center, they are reckless drivers. If they bump the sides, they have had a wreck. For the first two weeks, the children should have dotted lines to follow in order to develop the idea of what the "middle of the road" means. The "road" should be the width of a ruler.

1. For the first week make lines similar to Figure 1-2. They are the width of the master and have three or more similar ones on the same page.

2. Follow the example in Figure 1-3 by drawing vertical lines about half the length of the paper. Put three on the top half and three on the bottom half of the page.

3. Use the same types of line drawings without using the dotted lines. (See Figure 1-4.)

4. Mix the two types for review.

5. During this week make any drawing requiring straight line executions by the students. Figure 1-5 shows a dot in each corner. Be sure to add this to encourage children to make straight lines around the corners.

6. Figure 1-6 shows the addition of curved lines. The dotted lines are added in this and in any new addition.

7. For review, mix the previous two types of drawings as shown in Figure 1-7.

8. Review all types that the children have done to this point. Evaluate each child's work to see if any repeat work needs to be done by any child before he progresses to the next level.

9. Make circular and straight line mazes similar to those in Figure 1-8.

10. Start all over again using the same types of lines but with less width. Occasionally add a circular or straight line maze and increase the difficulty of these as soon as

the children are capable of more difficult ones. The lines should now look similar to those in Figure 1-9.

11. Finally have the children tracing over short single lines similar to those in Figure 1-10.

12. As numerals, letters, and name writing is begun, have masters ready with examples similar to those in Figure 1-11.

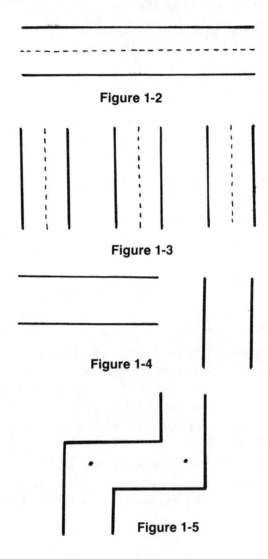

**Figure 1-2**

**Figure 1-3**

**Figure 1-4**

**Figure 1-5**

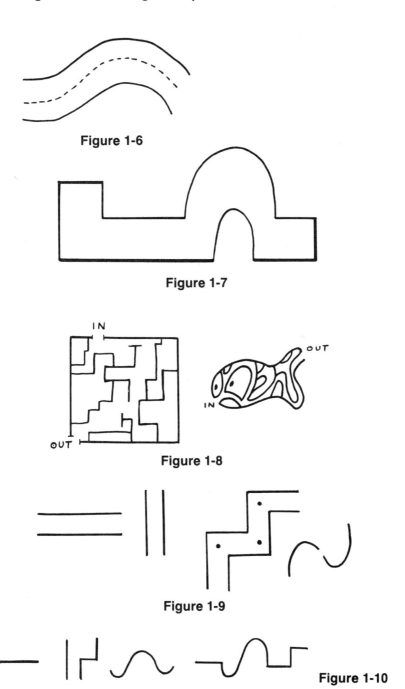

Figure 1-6

Figure 1-7

Figure 1-8

Figure 1-9

Figure 1-10

**Figure 1-11**

All the other activities in this book stress the development of coordination. Kindergarteners are engaged in active learning situations, all of which are valuable in the maturation processes involved in physical and mental growth. Watching this continuous process brings joy to any kindergarten teacher. Enjoy yourself!

# 2

## Exceptional Writing Skills: The Final Objective of Coordination Development

### How Writing Experiences Can Become Rewarding Exercises

Writing can either be one of the most exciting and meaningful experiences that students have, or it can be one of the most frustrating.

All writing experiences must be backed by sufficient fine motor development to ensure adequate eye-hand coordination. Following ample large and small coordination activities, many experiences involving as many of the five senses as possible are provided for the students. After writing is begun, a continuous reinforcement process must be perpetuated to insure that the children continuously adhere to correct writing procedures.

You have the responsibility of requiring your children to write with their dominant hand, whether it be the left or right hand. You must also help some children develop a preference for a particular hand. When handedness is established, and sufficient motor control is attained, writing experiences can be exciting and rewarding.

## Successful Performance Methods for Developing Pre-Writing Skills

You are encouraged to add to the cosmos of exercises in this chapter, changing them to meet your needs and situations. You are teaching individuals, and every group of individuals has its own personalities and needs. Keep a card file of all activities, adding improvements or changes as your group indicates the need.

A language background must be established before any of these activities or any others in this book can be carried out by the children.

### #1. "Action Numerals"

*Objectives:*

1. To recognize numeral name, shape, and set number.
2. To learn starting place, direction to proceed, and stopping place.
3. To develop visual discrimination for specific numerals.
4. To reinforce a left-to-right sequencing pattern.
5. To develop large motor coordination.

*Procedure:*

You should write very large numerals on the ground with a stick. If there is no ground area large enough, write them on a large area of blacktop. Or, if necessary, write them on a large strip of butcher paper to be used inside. Each one should be written on an individual sheet of paper.

Place these written numerals in a circular fashion so you and the children may stand in the center to watch the proceedings. If you use all the numerals to ten, have a definite opening between the one and the ten to magnify the ordering process.

Have one child stand at the top of numeral one—where you would ordinarily start writing it—two children stand at the starting place for two, and so on. You may want to start with only three or four numerals, as you will have to use children more than once.

Give each group an activity to perform, to which they react with the appropriate activity. They should also say the way to make their numeral as they perform. The following are examples of the types of activities and approximate voice replies.

1. You tell the child on numeral one to skip. He says, "I skip down to make the one."

2. Numeral two hops and says, "We hop around in a half circle and go straight back to make a two."

3. Numeral three walks and says, "We walk around in a half circle, go back (here the last child becomes the first), and around in a half circle again."

4. Two children stand at the starting place for four with two at the top of the crossing vertical line. The first two jump and say, "We jump down and straight back to make a chair shape." The next two jump and say, "We jump straight down across the chair bottom to finish the four."

5. All five children stand at the starting place. Three run and say, "We run straight down, go back, and then around in a half circle." The other two run and say, "We run straight back at the top to finish the five."

6. Numeral six hops on one foot and says, "We hop down and then curve around to make a circle at the bottom of the six."

7. Numeral seven tiptoes and says, "We tiptoe straight over and then turn and go down in a slant to make the seven."

8. Numeral eight waddles as a duck and says, "We waddle

around and then around the other way and then up to the starting place to make the eight."

9. Numeral nine walks happily and says, "We walk happily all the way around to make an oval shape and then straight down to make a nine."

10. Numeral ten takes baby steps, with five on the one and five on the zero. Those on the one say, "We take baby steps straight down to make the one of the ten." Those on the zero say, "We take baby steps and go all the way around in a circle to make the zero of the ten."

If you wish, do the above one at a time as they are being introduced. Have them written on large sheets of butcher paper and have each child perform each numeral, doing different types of activities. Take several days to complete each numeral if necessary.

## #2. "Active Letters"

*Objectives:*

1. To recognize letter name and shape. (You may want to use sound and shape, or both.)
2. To learn the starting place, direction to proceed, and stopping place for writing each letter.
3. To develop visual discrimination for each letter.
4. To develop left-to-right sequencing.
5. To develop large motor coordination.

*Procedure:*

To perform the letters, choose only a few letters to do at a time, or do each as it is introduced. Have only as many children performing each as are needed. For instance, for the small *a*, one child is sufficient, while for the capital *A*, three children are needed—two for the vertical lines and one for the horizontal. Again, have the children say the way they make the letter. Using *a* as an example, the child says as he hops, (for example) "I hop all the way around in a circle and then go straight down to make the small *a*." When the children voice the directions, and they always should, the direction becomes a part of their memory when they need it for writing on paper. Make up directions for each letter and teach them to the children as they perform them. Be sure that you always tell them the same way every time. Write them on a file card to use until you have a system completely in mind. A different direction each time confuses children and hinders the learning process.

#### #3. "I Can Numerals"

*Objectives:*

1. To develop a relationship between the set number and the numeral.
2. To develop large muscle coordination.
3. To develop left-to-right sequencing.

*Procedure:*

Assign one child for each numeral by giving each a numeral written on both sides of a nine- by twelve-inch sheet of paper. The numeral on both sides allows the child to see it without turning it around. First, have the children put themselves in a left-to-right order from one to ten. (This is valuable at any time to reinforce left-to-right sequencing without any other activity.)

You then ask each child to show his numeral and perform an activity. Each child must decide for himself how many times he is to perform an activity. The following are examples of the types of activities you might choose.

1. "One, skip rope." The child performs and says, "I can skip rope one time."
2. "Two, take giant steps." (Each child performs and tells what he is doing for this and all the following.)
3. "Three, bounce the ball."
4. "Four, jump as a kangaroo."

5. "Five, hop as a rabbit."

6. "Six, hop on one foot."

7. "Seven, walk as an elephant."

8. "Eight, jump over the block."

9. "Nine, hop on one foot then the other."

10. "Ten, bounce as a ball."

Repeat the sequence with different children and different directions.

As the children progress, have all performing the same activity for each numeral.

### #4. "Savory Letters or Numerals"

*Objectives:*

1. To reinforce the correct procedure for writing letters and numerals.

2. To develop motor coordination necessary for writing.

3. To develop a visual relationship between the symbol name and its representative shape.

*Procedure:*

Use a large sheet of clean butcher paper or other material, changing or cleaning after each group. Sprinkle a layer of sugar on the surface, large enough for you and five or six children to work around. When making the symbols, the children should write the figure, say how to write it, pronounce its name, and eat the sugar that has adhered to their finger. They always find a way to have a surplus to eat!

Work on only one numeral or letter at a time, and never a numeral and letter together. However, you can review symbols that have already been introduced. At this level of learning, the children are only ready for one new abstract symbol at a time, and you must be sure that they learn each before proceeding.

This does not mean that every child will master every symbol, but that most children will.

Using the same objectives and procedures, change the substance to salt, instant pudding mixture, or any other substance that you find is exceptionally pleasing.

## Using Art to Enhance Pre-Writing Experiences

Colorful and meaningful art activities are the center of most kindergarten experiences because of their ability to increase fine motor control. Learning to write can be fun when connected with something that is pretty and exciting to do.

#5. "Scrapbook Symbols"

*Objectives:*

1. To develop small motor coordination through cutting and pasting.
2. To develop a sense of directionality for each symbol.
3. To develop a relationship between the written symbol and its name.

*Procedure:*

Using twelve-by eighteen-inch colored construction paper, make each child a scrapbook, one sheet for each numeral, plus two for covers, and likewise for the letters. As the children study each numeral or letter, have large, nine-inch long symbols dittoed on other construction paper for the children to cut and paste to the top of the scrapbook page. These should be at least one inch or more in width to facilitate cutting and pasting. At the bottom of the large sheet, under the symbol, staple a sheet of paper on which you have dittoed the following, or similar material. (See Figure 2-1.)

1. A hollow symbol with a dotted line to trace. Have the starting place marked with a dot or $x$.

2. A dotted symbol to be traced.

3. One beginning symbol only, with students supplying copies.

4. A symbol beginning only.

5. An empty space where a picture representing the set number, or letter sound, is drawn.

**Figure 2-1**

Each page may take several days to complete, using different lines of work each day for review. When the scrapbooks are completed, the children have nice booklets to take home. The covers of the booklets may be decorated with each of the numerals or letters as they are studied. When completed, each booklet will have one of each of the symbols represented inside. These would be even prettier if the children could use different colored felt pens for making the symbols on the covers.

## #6. "Tissue Paper Symbols"

*Objectives:*

1. To obtain a lovely representative of each letter or numeral. These are pretty for bulletin boards.
2. To develop the fine motor coordination needed for writing.
3. To reinforce the visual representatives for the symbols and the respective names for each.
4. To learn the correct procedure for making the symbol.

*Procedure:*

Cut out many circles of colored tissue paper, about an inch in diameter. You can cut through a whole quire at a time, so this is not as difficult as it may seem. When the circles are cut out, have each child make a representation of the letter or numeral being studied on a nine- by twelve-inch sheet of white construction paper. The tissue paper is gently dabbed in the center in a mixture of glue and water. It is then placed in the arrangement of the symbol as large as the children can make it. These make lovely decorations for the room, and everyone can be equally proud of their own. If you wish, the children may make the symbol only on the top half of the paper while making the representative set number at the bottom using the circles. These can be put in any pattern the children choose. The same can be done for the letters, with an outline of an object made to represent the sound of each. By choosing simple objects, such as an apple for *a*, ball for *b*, candy cane for *c*, doughnut for *d*, etc., the process will not be too complicated. When adding representations for the symbols, you may wish to use a larger sheet of construction paper.

## #7. "Curly Cues"

*Objectives:*

1. To obtain a pretty representation of the letters and numerals.

2. To develop visual perception for the symbol and its name.

3. To develop the fine motor coordination necessary to write.

*Procedure:*

No doubt your school has received materials from supply houses packed in the little squiggly pieces of foam. Never let them be thrown away. They are useful for so many art projects. It is best, for this project, to draw a large representation of the symbol on a nine- by twelve-inch sheet of colored construction paper. You should make a light pencil drawing, as it is simple to cover. Give each group of children a bunch of the squiggle characters and let them glue (not paste) them on top of the drawn symbol. These make lovely bulletin board displays, while teaching a valuable lesson. If the symbol is a numeral, a representative set may be added to the page. If it is a letter, a representative sound symbol in outline form may be added. For adding representations, larger sheets of paper should be used.

## How to Make Symbols Come to Life

When students are learning any symbol, it is an abstract term to them. This is what makes learning letters and numerals so difficult for children. In order to make these characters come to life, in a manner of speaking, each should be treated as much like a "person" as possible. Therefore, this activity should take top priority when children are learning the abstract symbols of letters and numerals.

#8. "People Numerals"

*Objectives:*

1. To give character to the symbol being studied.

2. To enable the children to always remember where the beginning and ending of a symbol are located.

3. To associate the name with the symbol.

4. To develop fine motor coordination.

*Procedure:*

Following the activity portion of this lesson, have each child write the symbol in question in the center of a 9- x 12-in. sheet of white construction paper. You should have a sample for them to follow on display. Let the children write the symbols themselves if they can, using brightly colored felt markers. They love to use them, and they add color and width to this experience.

Since there will be a stick figure when completed, one color should be chosen for the symbol which is not repeated in the drawing. This could be black or brown. Once the symbol is drawn, the head is added; then the arms and hands at the sides; finally the legs and feet, or shoes, at the bottom. The children may want to add other features later. See the illustration for ideas for the drawings and the character portrayals. Here are the representations I have used. You may want to change some or make up new ones.

1. *Numeral one.* Have all the children act out a tall, straight person. They then draw features on their tall, straight numeral one.

2. *Numeral two.* The children portray a praying figure, curving their body as they kneel and sit back.

3. *Numeral three.* The children portray a baby playing "patty cake."

4. *Numeral four.* The drawing is of a child rowing a boat. However, the children may decide how they want to act it out. After all, kindergarteners are very ingenious characters! One way of doing this is to have a child sit on one chair with his feet on a stool or block holding a yardstick between his knees for the vertical line. Or, another child may stand on his knees behind the legs of the first child to show the vertical line.

5. *Numeral five.* The drawing is of a fireman with the bill of his hat behind his head at the neck. He is rolling up a

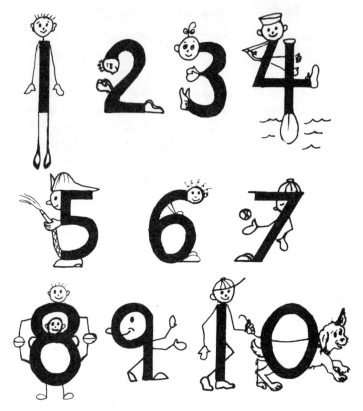

**Figure 2-2**

hose. The portrayal may be done with a jump rope, or, the children may think of a better way to show the numeral five.

6. *Numeral six.* The drawing is of an acrobat who can fold his legs behind him into a circular shape. Let the children think of ways to portray him.

7. *Numeral seven.* I always tell the children that seven is the shy one. He always puts his hat on before anything else. He can be portrayed by placing a cap with a bill on the head, or a fireman's hat placed on backward, while pretending to walk against a strong wind to get the slant in the vertical line.

8. *Numeral eight.* The drawing is again of an acrobat who can get into the position of an eight. Since the children will not be able to do this, have about three team up to decide on ways to act it out.

9. *Numeral nine.* This is the one we call "Limberneck." He can turn his head all the way around while standing straight and tall. If this is tried, be sure the children do not try to force another's head to the back. This may also be drawn and portrayed as a child holding a balloon behind his shoulder. This is much easier to demonstrate, but the children like to remember "Ole Nine, the limberneck."

10. *Numeral ten.* Here we have a child leading a dog on a leash. This should prove to be an interesting demonstration as children think of ways to show the ten.

After they are finished drawing their characters, have all the children come together and decide on names for all their numeral characters. This will help them remember the symbols forever. They will have ten new friends with whom they can have fun and exciting times.

#### #9. "People Letters"

*Objectives:*

1. To give character to an abstract symbol.
2. To enable children to remember where to start and stop when writing each letter.
3. To associate the name with the symbol.
4. To develop fine motor control.

*Procedure:*

The procedure is the same as for numerals. The letter may become the head in some cases and the whole body in others. For instance, the small *a* is used as the head of the character. Using the capital *A*, you have a head at the top and a body and legs at the bottom. The children can add a hat, face, arms, hands, and shoes. Allow the children to help you decide on ways to demonstrate each character before it is drawn. Give each character a name after the drawing is completed.

## Successful Ways to Cultivate Symbol Writing Skills

The end results of the evolving methods used in pre-writing skills in which kindergarten children must be engaged are readable and correctly formed symbols. It is unreasonable to assume that every child in kindergarten will have progressed to this stage, but it is a goal worth seeking.

On pages 204-211 in my previous book, you will find the method by which I have taught kindergarten children to write for years.* Other methods for developing correct writing habits are equally important as reinforcers. The following are simple and effective ways to augment your writing program. The objectives are the same for all the activities.

*Objectives:*

1. To offer practice in writing the symbols.
2. To develop fine motor coordination necessary for writing on paper.
3. To insure that students are learning the correct procedure for writing the symbols.
4. To further the recognition of each symbol and to relate each to its name.

#10. "Numeral Maze"

*Procedure:*

On a master set, draw as many numerals as you wish to put on a page by forming a double line and closed ends, each sepa-

---

*Lewallen, *Op. Cit.*

rated from the other. (See Figure 2-3.) Put a dot or small *x* at the starting place for each numeral. Have the children trace down through the middle of each with a crayon. Your first master set for this work should contain dotted lines for the children to follow. Subsequent papers would leave the line out. Different colored crayons are used for each symbol.

**Figure 2-3**

## #11. "Letter Maze"

*Procedure:*

Use the same procedure for this activity as was used in the preceding one. The first copy should have only one letter represented, but you may add to it in subsequent lessons as more letters are learned.

## #12. "Numeral Figure Ground Maze"

*Procedure:*

Put as many of the same numeral on one master as you think your children can manage. Add more as they progress, and add more than one numeral, later. Each numeral overlaps the other, and the children must find each and trace over it. Have the children use a different colored crayon for each numeral they find. These numerals, too, should be enclosed with dotted lines to be traced. Later, the dotted lines may be left out and the children can trace down through the middle of the closed numeral. (See Figure 2-4.)

**Figure 2-4**

#13. "Letter Figure Ground Maze"

*Procedure:*

Follow the same procedure as for the preceding activity.

Other chapters have other ideas for writing activities. You are encouraged to use as many of them as you can in order to develop the necessary coordination for future writing experiences. Have fun!

# 3

---

## A Galaxy of Ways to Help Kindergarteners Acquire Pre-Reading Skills

---

### The Importance of the Kindergarten Teacher's Task

Guiding children in the acquisition of pre-reading skills means that you must be concerned with the development of every attribute mentioned in this book—perception, large and small motor coordination, self-control, incentive, language development, cooperation, reasoning, etc. Pre-reading *is* the development of these attributes to the point of such refinement that the children will be able to grasp the abstract concepts of letters and words when they are finally introduced. However, if you do this, you should not be concerned with teaching kindergarteners to read. Building a firm foundation on which reading skills will be taught is by far the most important task in teaching children to read.

Although pre-reading is the acquisition of all these skills, for the purposes of this book, activities involving the learning of letters, sounds, children's names, and the perceptions involved in learning word differences, also usually taught in kindergarten, will be the basis for the activities in this chapter.

## Methods Through Which Learning Letters Takes Place

### #1. "Lay-On Letters"

*Objectives:*

1. To develop perception for letter shapes and differences in letters.
2. To increase background information concerning pre-reading.
3. To learn to recognize beginning letters of the name.

*Procedure:*

This activity can be used as a prelude or continuation of Activity #2 in Chapter 2. It can be used at the beginning of school when you are teaching children to recognize their name; later in the year when they are learning letter names and sounds; and when they are learning how to write the letters.

On a sheet of butcher paper three to four feet in length, write a large representation of the letter needed. This is then laid on the floor. If you are working on a single letter name, three or more copies of the same letter would allow more children to participate at one time. If it is being used for names at the beginning of the year and you wish to teach children what their beginning letter is like, write one letter for each child.

The children can do several things with these letters. These are only a few suggestions. Save the letters for other uses; when rolled up, they will take little space.

1. Form the letter with the body laying on top of the written letter.

2. Curl up inside any opening. Examples are *a, d,* and *p.*

3. Put as much of the body around the letter as possible.

4. Trace it with the hands and/or feet.

5. Perform actions over the letters. (See Chapter 2.)

Upper-case letters are used for name beginnings. Do not allow your students to write their complete name in capital letters.

## #2. "Letter Jungle"

*Objectives:*

1. To increase perception for specific letters.

2. To develop eye-hand coordination skills.

3. To reinforce proper procedures for writing letters.

4. To learn letter names and/or sounds.

*Procedure:*

On a master set, draw a scribble design of any sort that will best serve the letter, or letters, you wish the children to learn. (See Figure 3-1.) Make one master for each letter as it is studied. Combine letters later for review. The children are to find all the symbols on the page and trace over them with a crayon.

If you wish, you may collect the sheets each day and add them to other alphabet papers for a booklet. Entitle the booklet. "My Alphabet Jungle Book."

**Figure 3-1**

## #3. "Clay Letters"

*Objectives:*

1. To increase knowledge of letter formations.
2. To develop fine motor control.
3. To increase perception for specific letters.
4. To have an enjoyable time while learning.

*Procedure:*

Allow the children to develop their own method for forming letters of clay. If they have difficulty, here are two methods they may use.

1. Roll out long, thin strips of clay. Take a small piece and form the letter or letters. Do not discourage children who wish to put these in alphabetical order, as some children will have advanced to this phase of learning.

2. Roll out a flat piece of clay with some round object. With a small object such as a pencil, stick, or tongue depressor, draw the letter shapes in the clay. As you go around the room, ask several children how they made the letter. Have them trace over the indented letter with their finger as they explain the procedure. This allows them to feel the letter with their hands.

At another time, you may have the children using either method followed by a clay example of an object that begins with the sound the letter makes.

## #4. "Bingo"

*Objectives:*

1. To reinforce letter recognition.
2. To reinforce letter sounds.
3. To play an enjoyable game.

4. To develop perception for likenesses and differences in letters and sounds.

*Procedure:*

Make Bingo cards of tagboard or posterboard. You may make the cards with nine, sixteen, or twenty-five spaces depending on the maturity of your students. Do not use a heading such as "Bingo" across the top of the rows. You may or may not use a free space, and if you do, it can go anywhere on the card. You may use all the same letters on all the cards, putting them in different spaces, or, you may use some different letters. Six to eight cards are sufficient for each set you make. An aide, parent, or older student can then take students aside and call letters, or sounds, for them. I play with my children. When they win, they get to call. When I win, I call. They learn from calling the letters for others.

When using this card for sounds, call the letter sound instead of the letter name.

Laminate all of your Bingo cards on both sides, and they will last for years. For more on Bingo games, refer to my previous book, mentioned before. There are innumerable games you can make for kindergarten use.

## #5. "Books"

*Objectives for procedures 5-6:*

1. To reinforce letter names.
2. To develop perception for likenesses and differences in letters.
3. To enjoy a game.

*Procedure:*

Buy blank cards and write the same letter on two of them. The letter should be written on the cards as shown in Figure 3-2 in order for the children to see the letter upright regardless of which way it is turned.

About thirty cards are sufficient for three or four players. Too many cards in little hands are hard to manage. The game is played as "Books" is played, with each child trying to gather the most books by calling from other children. Again, it is best to have someone oversee the game, especially since some of the children may need help with some of the letter names.

If you are studying sounds, the children will call for cards by letter sounds rather than by name.

**Figure 3-2**

### #6. "Old Maid"

*Procedure:*

Draw several different funny faces and add one to the deck of cards used for "Books." The children can then name the game to match the face "for the day." It might be "Grumpy," "Smiley," "The Monster," "Sourpuss," "Angel," etc. Kindergarteners love these characters, and they add excitement to learning the letters.

### #7. "Match-Up"

*Objectives:*

1. To develop powers of concentration.

2. To increase perception for letter likenesses and differences.

3. To reinforce letter names through an enjoyable game.

*Procedure:*

Use the same cards you made for "Books" and let the children turn them face down on a table. They turn them over two at each turn, trying to match the most sets. If they match a set, they get another turn. The one with the most sets wins the game. This is played just as the games you buy of Memory.™ It is excellent for building concentration, and it can be made up of most any subject in kindergarten.

## Ways to Discover How Sounds Work for Us

Without the sounds that letters represent, there would be no need for letters. Teaching this abstract concept to kindergarten children is not the easiest task you can undertake. The following examples are only a few of the many activities throughout this book which promote the sounds letters make.

#8. "What Is Your Sound?"

*Objectives for procedures 8-11:*

1. To teach children discrimination for the different letters.

2. To teach letter sounds.

3. To develop perception for sounds of letters.

4. To develop the concept that all words are letters spoken as sounds.

*Procedure:*

The day you are introducing a new letter and its sound, write the letter on a tag for each child. As the children come to school, pin the tag on them with a safety pin. Straight pins get lost too quickly and may stick inquisitive fingers. At the end of the day, make sure they take the pin off to return to you and take the tag home with them.

As you pin the tag on each child, tell him the name of the letter, that it is his name for the day, and that his sound is____. Then ask each one, "What is your name?" They respond with the letter name. You ask, "What sound do you make?" They respond with the sound. Do this whenever you have a spare moment with either individuals or groups.

This activity should be used in conjunction with other letter- and sound-learning activities.

### #9. "Hide and Seek"

*Procedure:*

Before the children come to school for the day, place several cards (large size) that display the letter and sound of the day around the room on objects that begin with that sound. Most should be in sight, but a few can be partially hidden. When the children are *all* seated for beginning activities, tell them that you have hidden some letters, and that if anyone finds one and can tell you its name and the sound of the object it represents, they may get it and bring it to you. As hands go up, choose children one by one to find a letter, say the object's name, and tell what the beginning sound is. About ten cards for each sound is sufficient. When you have letters for which you have difficulty finding objects, put up pictures of the objects, such as zoo, zebra, zero, zipper, etc., for the letter *z*.

### #10. "Letter-Sound Match-Up"

*Procedure:*

As a review on the following day, place the same letter around the room but on objects that do not begin with the sound. Tell the children that they may find a letter if they can also find an object that goes with the sound that letter represents. They should then place the letter on the correct object.

This is a good way to review several sounds, and it may be used later for evaluation.

## #11. "I Spy"

*Procedure:*

Another follow-up activity after letters are introduced and placed on objects around the room is "I Spy." This time no letters are used. The children are to look around the room and find objects that begin with the particular sound, then briefly describe it. For instance, if the letter is *s*, a child might say, "I see something that begins with (s). It has two holes for fingers." If the other children do not guess *scissors*, he can continue giving the attributes of scissors until they do. For instance, he might say that the object is shiny, made of metal, has two parts, and, finally, it cuts paper.

This not only helps to develop sound discrimination, but it also develops language skills. Follow this same procedure when reviewing several sounds at a time.

## #12. "Sound and Letter Association"

*Objectives:*

1. To reinforce the concept that letters are representatives for sounds.
2. To reinforce writing skills.
3. To develop small motor coordination.
4. To increase language skills.
5. To develop auditory and visual perception.

*Procedure:*

On tagboard or posterboard, cut cards approximately six by twelve inches. Make dotted letters for children to trace between two wide lines, with a dotted line in the middle, as primary writing paper is made. Place pictures that represent the sound of the letter at the left side. (See Figure 3-3.) On the back of the upper-case letter, make the corresponding lower-case letter. Cover these cards with plastic or have them laminated for many years of use. The children should use suitable markers to trace and write the letters. Be sure the markings are easily removed from the plastic cover.

Another way to do the same thing is to get wide-lined writing sheets of paper, the kind especially made for primary school children, and put a sheet on both sides of a piece of tagboard cut to the same size. After writing the letters and drawing a picture to represent the sound, laminate the cards.

**Figure 3-3**

#### #13. "Matching"

*Objectives for procedures 13-14:*

1. To reinforce sound discrimination.
2. To associate sound with letter.
3. To develop eye-hand coordination.

*Procedure:*

On a sheet of tagboard, draw or paste small pictures to represent sounds of letters that you will place to the right of each picture. (See Figure 3-4.) The letters to the right should contain at least two that have the sound of the picture represented. These cards should be laminated so the children can underline the correct letters or cross out the incorrect ones. This activity should be used in the latter part of the year. It is excellent for evaluation purposes. Make several cards that represent all the sounds.

**Figure 3-4**

## #14. "Picture Matching"

*Procedure:*

Make the same type of cards as in the preceding exercise, but put one letter to the left of each row followed by about four small pictures, with at least two representing the beginning sound of the letter. (See Figure 3-5.) After laminating the cards, the children mark those that begin with the sound of the letter at the left, or they cross out the incorrect sounds. This is another good evaluation activity.

**Figure 3-5**

## How to Reinforce Correct Letter Ordering in Words

Children with poor visual perception often have difficulty putting the letters of their names or other words in the proper order. Add the following activities to those you are using.

## #15. "Letter Line-Up"

*Objectives:*

1. To teach children to recognize their names.

2. To develop perception for likenesses and differences in names.

3. To develop concept for letter shapes and sizes.

4. To begin the concept of sequencing.

*Procedure:*

This activity is to be used at the beginning of the school year when you want children to recognize their names. It can also be used as a visual perception test.

Write about six children's names on nine- by twelve-inch construction paper, one letter to each sheet. Write the letter on both sides so the children holding the letters can see them without turning them away from others. Pass out the letters you have written, being sure that you have sufficient letters for all six names. Some letters may be used more than once, but if you have more children than letters, make duplicate ones anyway.

Write the complete name on another sheet of paper which you hold up in front of the group. Ask if anyone can recognize it as his name. If not, tell him, and have that person line up children who hold the letters of his name in front of you while he looks at the letters on your card. Since you are standing behind the others, the child who is operating can always see the order of his name. If he is successful, make a quick note on a card and go on to the next child. If he is not successful, make a note of his mistakes, study them later, and devise ways to remedy the perceptual problem. Continue this activity throughout the week until all children have had the opportunity to form their names. This activity can be used with any concept involving the ordering process.

Save these cards and use them later to see how many children can order the letters in their names without looking at a model.

### #16. "Word Match-Up"

*Objectives:*

1. To reinforce likenesses and differences in words.

2. To increase visual perception.

3. To reinforce the ordering and sequencing process.

4. To increase eye-hand coordination.

*Procedure:*

During the last third of the school year, after many visual discrimination exercises have been introduced and mastered, you will want to know if children can match words. Divide a twelve- by twelve-inch piece of tagboard into three-inch squares. Write a word in each box. Pictures that represent the sounds add to the beauty of the card. Use both sides and laminate for longer service. Make three- by three-inch matching cards with the same words written on them. Store the words in a small plastic box. The process requires children to match the smaller cards to the words on the larger board. (See Figure 3-6.)

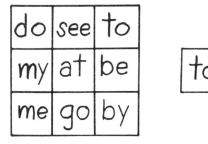

**Figure 3-6**

#17. "Name Scramble"

*Objectives for procedures 17-18:*

1. To reinforce proper letter sequencing in the name.

2. To learn how to form each letter.

3. To develop coordination for writing.

4. To discriminate one letter from another.

5. To discriminate letters belonging to one's own name.

*Procedure:*

On a master set write several letters on divided strips that contain two or three names of children per strip. Cut the strips and give each child the strip from which he can locate his name. Suppose you have these names:

| | |
|---|---|
| Tom | Sherrie |
| Marla | Kevin |
| Joyce | Joe |

Your master may have these scrambled letters:

S T h o e m r l r k i d e
M K a e r v l i a n
J a o g y b c o n e

You should write these in manuscript, as typing is too small for children of this age. You will notice that each child can sequentially form his name without running into the same letters again. However, your next master might look something like this: (Using the names of Joyce and Joe as examples.)

J a o g J o b y o c J e n e y

This is more difficult as the child must find the number of letters that form his name, and no more.

### #18. "Figure Ground Name Maze"

*Procedure:*

Write as many overlapping letters on a master set as you think your children can discriminate. (See Figure 3-7.) The letters you use should make up the names of some of the children. Make enough masters to include all children. Do not include letters that do not belong in a name. If some children have poor perception, put fewer names on the page for them. Have each child find only the letters for his name from the sheet. There may be several letters that belong to him, but he is to find only enough to correctly spell his name. They are to trace over the letters that belong to their name with a crayon, leaving others blank. If some energetic soul says that he can find other names, let him do so with a different colored crayon for each name. Those who can do so should now write the letters of their name in the correct order at the bottom of the page.

As children progress in discrimination, they could be given these same sheets and allowed to find as many names as they can, using different colored crayons for each. For this exercise, you should have all the names on display.

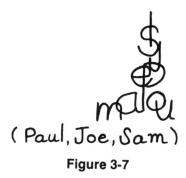

( Paul, Joe, Sam )

**Figure 3-7**

## How to Develop Discrimination for Letter Sizes

Just as children have difficulty with the order of letters in words, they also experience difficulty with the different letter sizes. Knowing which letters are tall or which extend below lines is difficult for even the most mature youngsters.

### #19. "Where Is It?"

*Objectives:*

1. To develop visual discrimination.
2. To develop skills necessary for reading and writing.

*Procedure:*

On nine- by twelve-inch construction paper draw four wide lines as if you were making writing paper. The second line is dotted as writing paper is. Use wide felt marking pens for the lines. Using water colors because of their light tone, paint between the lines as Figure 3-8 shows. Cover this with plastic or laminate it.

As letters are introduced to the children, with a plastic marking pen write each one in order for the children to see if it (1) stands tall, reaching into the sky; (2) if it is short, staying only in the green area; or (3) if it grows below ground in the brown area. If it is in the green and blue as a *b* would be, have all the children stand. If it is only in the green area as a *c* would be, have them all sit. If it is partially in the brown area as a *g* would be, have the children lie down on their stomachs with elbows on the floor and head resting on the hands.

When showing several letters to the children, name one group of children *trees* for the tall letters: the next group can be *shrubs* or other low plants that children suggest; and the last group can be *radishes*, carrots, tulips, etc.—any plant that grows from a bulb or produces food underground. When you write tall letters, the "trees" stand, For short letters, the "shrubs" sit. For underground root plants, the group lays down as suggested.

If you make several of these painted sheets and laminate them, the children having difficulty writing the letters can use them as aids.

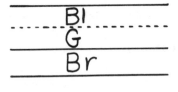

**Figure 3-8**

### #20. "Musical Letters"

*Objectives:*

1. To develop auditory discrimination for musical tones.

2. To develop the concept of high, middle, and low.
3. To develop the idea that some letters are high, or tall, some are middle sized, and some are low on lines.

*Procedure:*

This activity is good for developing musical discrimination for different notes, but it is used here to emphasize the different appearances of letters.

Find a simple piece of music that has specific accented high and low beats with several regular beats, or record your own. All you need to do is pick out three notes on the piano—one high, one low, and one in the middle range—and play them in mixed order.

As in the previous activity, name your three groups, *trees*, *shrubs*, and *carrots*, or other names the children prefer. In front of each group place a large sheet of paper on which you have written all the letters they are to represent. Tell the children that when they hear the high notes, the "trees" stand; show them why on their letter chart. If they hear low notes, the "carrots" lie down; if they hear middle notes, the "shrubs" sit.

The first part of your recording should have a longer length of time for each tone in order to acquaint each group with the tone it represents. For instance, using *h* for high notes, *m* for middle, and *l* for the low notes, start your recording something like this:

*m m m m m m m m m m m m m m m m m l l l l l l l l l l l l l l l l l h h h h h h h h h h h h h h* then go into something like this: *hhh mmmm l hhhh lllll mmmmmm hhhh lll*, etc. Have all children sitting in chairs. When they perform, they do so on the floor.

Other activities that develop reading readiness skills needed for future reading success are described throughout this book. Since everything we do in kindergarten is a prelude to reading, writing, and mathematics—and since these require similar background skills—almost any activity in this book is appropriate for pre-reading advancement.

# 4

## Promoting Future Math Skills Through Purposeful Pre-Math Performances

### How Math Affects Kindergarteners

Math is similar to reading in that it is affected by almost every phase of kindergarten training. Very few things we do throughout the day are not affected in some way by math concepts, particularly math language. How often we use the words "little," "big," "round," "red," "green," "short," "many," "few," etc! They are all words that affect a child's understanding of math concepts. For our purposes as kindergarten teachers, building a foundation for future math skills by teaching children the basic math language is of prime importance. This includes all the words affecting size, shape, and color as well as simple counting, the names of the numerals, and the set number in corresponding size.

Emphasize words related to math concepts in other activities. Rarely will you find an activity that does not include some aspect that is associated with mathematics.

## Unique Ways to Promote Counting Skills

Learning to count may be easy for most children, but learning that each numeral represents a specific number is another concept. Until a child can correlate the spoken or written numeral to a specific set, there is no real understanding. All counting activities should incorporate these two concepts.

### #1. "Numeral Hide and Seek"

*Objectives for procedures 1-3:*

1. To develop counting skills.
2. To develop language skills.
3. To teach that numeral names represent sets of things.

*Procedure:*

This is played as Activity #9 in Chapter 3. Before the children come to school for the day, place cards on which you have written some numerals around the room on objects that number as many as the numeral represents. When the children come, tell them that you have hidden some numerals. They may get a card from its hiding place if they can count the number of objects it is standing near. This means that they do not have to recognize the numeral at this time. You may add that in a later game. Do this for two or three days until the children are becoming familiar with sets and numeral representation.

### #2. "Numeral Match-Up"

*Procedure:*

This activity should follow the preceding one. Before the children get to school, place the numeral cards around the room, but do not put them with the correct set. The children must now be able to recognize the numeral and the set that it represents. This will be more difficult, but some children will be able to do it. Continue this at regular intervals as a test to see who really can match the numeral to its set.

### #3. "Set I Spy"

*Procedure:*

Instead of asking children to count objects, play the game "I Spy." The object is to have the children look around the room, find a set of objects (from one to ten), and say, "I see something. There are__ objects." The other children try to guess. If they cannot, the child describes some of the attributes of the objects until someone guesses.

### #4. "Counting Rope Jumps"

*Objectives:*

1. To develop sequential counting skills.
2. To have fun.
3. To develop coordination.
4. To develop language skills.

*Procedure:*

By springtime many kindergarten children like to play jump-rope games while singing counting rhymes. It is an excellent way to promote counting skills without the teacher asking them. Other activities mentioned in Chapter 1 are particularly suitable for developing counting skills. For instance, take ten hops, eight steps, three skips, etc.

### #5. "How Many?"

*Objectives:*

1. To develop counting skills,

2. To develop tactile perception.

3. To arouse curiosity and to make learning fun.

*Procedure:*

In a small box with low sides, put from one to ten objects. Bring some little things from home to arouse the children's curiosity for what they will find each day. Put the smaller box under a larger one by turning the larger box over it. Cut a hole in one side of the larger box from which the children can take out the objects.

A child stands behind the box with one hand inside, feeling each object before he takes it out and describing its feel to the others. Everyone tries to guess what it is, including the person at the box. If no one guesses right away, tell the child to take the object out to see what it is. As the items are taken from the box, they should be counted to see how many things were in the secret box for the day. Have a different number each day and let different children have a turn at the box.

#### #6. "Dot-to-Dot"

*Objectives;*

1. To develop numeral sequencing.

2. To increase recognition of numerals.

3. To reinforce counting skills.

*Procedure:*

There are many coloring books on the market with dot-to-dot sequencing. Buy some that begin with ten numerals and slowly progress upward. You should then make a master of the ones you want to use. After you've passed them out to the children, they should draw in the picture and color it. Be sure that the pictures are very simple and do not add extraneous material. Let the children add any external characteristics if they wish.

## #7. "Finger Play"

*Objectives:*

1. To develop language skills.
2. To increase counting skills.
3. To enjoy an activity.

*Procedure:*

I am sure that every kindergarten teacher uses finger plays. Their benefit for counting and developing language skills cannot be minimized. Any finger play or song is delightful and increases proficiency in many areas. Use fingers to demonstrate the following finger play written by me. Later, let the children act it out as they say it.

"One, two, three, four, five little friends,
Opened their mouths to grin.
But to their surprise,
In popped five lady bugs, *very much alive!*
The mouths closed;
The lady bugs cried;
But quick as a wink,
Those mouths opened wide!
Out flew one, two, three, four, five.
H-m-mmmmm, everyone is *still* alive."

## Reinforcing Numeral Names and Set Numbers

## #8. "Scramble"

*Objectives for procedures 8-9:*

1. To develop perception for correct numeral sequencing.
2. To have fun.
3. To reinforce set ordering according to size.

*Procedure:*

Write each numeral to ten, one to each sheet of nine- by twelve-inch construction paper. Be sure to write it on both sides. Give each numeral to a different child and have all stand in a semi-circle in front of the others. The semi-circle allows each of the group members to see each other. You have handed these out in scrambled order, and now you say, "The rest of us want to see how fast you get all the numerals in the proper order." And what a scramble! They love it and they are learning.

## #9. "Sets Scramble"

*Procedure:*

Use the same procedure as the preceding activity, but draw black circles on the construction paper to represent all the numerals to ten. Pass these out in scrambled order and have the children quickly put themselves in ascending order. This is more difficult, and children will have to stop and count many of the sets in order to know where they are to be placed. But continue this throughout the year and they will soon be able to recognize the sets quickly by their arrangement.

## #10. "Find the Numerals"

*Objectives for procedures 10-11:*

1. To increase preception for specific numerals.
2. To develop eye-hand coordination.
3. To reinforce numeral and matching set number.

*Procedure:*

On a master set make several of the same numeral. Later you can add several different numerals to each page. Draw a scribble design over the numerals. Do not make the numeral too difficult to find. (See Figure 4-1.) Have the children find and trace the numerals with a crayon. When more than one numeral is on the sheet, the children should use a different colored crayon for each.

**Figure 4-1**

## #11. "Find the Sets"

*Procedure:*

On a master set write a specific numeral at the top of the page; for example, 7. Now draw that many objects on the page, scribble over them, and have the children find them. They should trace over them with a crayon. (See Figure 4-2.)

## #12. "Bingo"

*Objectives for procedures 12-13:*

1. To reinforce numeral recognition.
2. To have fun while learning.
3. To reinforce set number for specific numerals.

*Procedure:*

Bingo games with numerals are very exciting to kindergarten children. You can have as few as nine spaces or as many as twenty-five on your bingo cards. They should be made of posterboard; the numerals that you want to reinforce should be written on them, then laminated. Counting chips of plastic or heavy

**Figure 4-2**

paper are your best covers. They are relatively inexpensive, and most kindergarten rooms have them anyway.

Towards the latter part of the year I have had a few children who knew their numerals well enough to play bingo on regular store-bought cards. They also could listen to a taped recording of the numbers called without help from others. They were watched but otherwise left alone.

### #13. "Sets Bingo"

*Procedure:*

A card with nine spaces is best for this bingo game. Draw circles with black markers in the spaces instead of numerals. Use only sets from one to ten, and if you study the zero, add empty sets. By placing the numerals in different spaces on your card and having a free space, you can make six or eight cards for a small group to play. The caller will have to remember that it will take the children longer to find the correct set because some will have to stop to count them. Eventually, if this game is played enough, the children will be able to recognize the sets quickly.

### #14. "Books"

*Objectives for procedures 14-17:*

1. To reinforce recognition of numerals and sets.

2. To have fun.

3. To encourage cooperation.

*Procedure:*

Make a deck of cards with two of the same numeral written on blank cards. See Activity 5 in Chapter 3 for making the cards. You may want to add all the numerals to twenty. The children then call from each other, trying to get the most sets of matching numerals.

You can also make a deck of cards with sets on them, but go no further than ten. For this deck, you should make at least four of each set. This will almost be necessary because of the limited range of numbers covered. The children play this game as they do the one with the numerals. If you wish to go to twenty with the numerals, make four of each for that game also.

You may also divide the cards, using two numerals and two set cards, and play the game by matching numeral and set number.

## #15. "Old Maid"

*Procedure:*

Use the same cards used for "Books" in the preceding games and add a fun card. (See Chapter 3) The children then play as they would play "Old Maid."

## #16. "Slap Jack"

*Procedure:*

Use the same cards as used in the preceding card games. Play the game as you would Slap Jack, but instead of slapping the Jack, the children slap any particular numeral or set number suggested for that day. In this game, all the cards are passed out to the players, who hold them face down in their hands. They each take turns laying down cards until the right one turns up. The first child to slap it gets all the cards in the pile. The winner is the one who ends up with all the cards. You may combine sets and numerals if you wish.

## #17. "Independent Sequencing"

*Procedure:*

Using the same cards as used in the card games, let two or three children arrange them in numerical order. In case of sets, they will order according to size. This is a quick testing device, yet, one that children enjoy doing. They can also match up cards that are alike. Or, they can match a set to the corresponding numeral.

## #18. "Match-Up"

*Objectives:*

1. To develop powers of concentration.
2. To increase understanding of numerals and sets.
3. To have fun while learning.

*Procedure:*

Use the same cards as in the card games and let the children play as in the game of "Match-Up," Activity #7 of Chapter 3. The set cards and numeral cards may be combined for a different game.

## #19. "Game Boards"

*Objectives:*

1. To develop powers of cencentration.
2. To increase language skills and one-to-one counting.
3. To increase cooperation.
4. To have fun while learning.

*Procedure:*

There are many easy game boards on the market with which kindergarten children can play. As they advance on the board, they must be able to count and follow instructions. Children love to be able to play games that they see older children in their families playing. It is a great incentive when they think that soon they will be able to play the ones they have at home. Some children are very good at complicated ones.

If you prefer, you can make the game boards yourself. This allows you the opportunity to include the material you want to reinforce in your classroom. When laminated, these boards will last for many years. My previous book explains in detail how to make these boards with suitable material for your classroom.*

## Building a Language Bank of Mathematical Terms

Without a linguistic background of the terms used in math, any problem solving becomes passive and a rote process. As kindergarten teachers, we are to lay the foundation for an active understanding of the procedures involved in mathematical equations.

### #20. "Shapes and Numerals"

*Objectives for procedures 20-21:*

1. To increase recognition of sets and numerals.
2. To increase recognition of shapes.
3. To reinforce language usage for shape names.

*Procedure:*

Cut out several cards of posterboard about ten by ten inches in size. On the left side put a set of shapes. To the right of this set make several numerals, with at least two that represent the set. (See Figure 4-3.) Laminate the boards and let the children mark the correct numeral for each set. Make different shapes for each

---

*Lewallen, *Op. Cit.*, Chapter 7.

set. Make enough boards so every shape and numeral is represented.

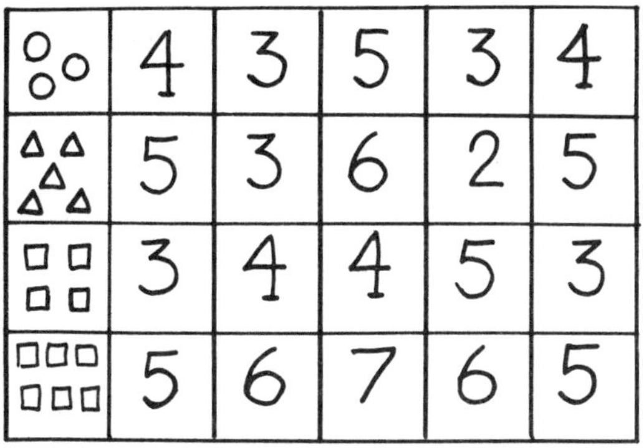

| | | | | | |
|---|---|---|---|---|---|
| ○○ ○ | 4 | 3 | 5 | 3 | 4 |
| △△ △ △△ | 5 | 3 | 6 | 2 | 5 |
| □ □ □ □ | 3 | 4 | 4 | 5 | 3 |
| □□□ □□□ | 5 | 6 | 7 | 6 | 5 |

**Figure 4-3**

## #21. "Numerals and Shapes"

*Procedure:*

This is the opposite of the previous activity and is made as it
is, except the numeral is placed at the left with several sets to
the right. The children mark the correct sets that match the
numeral. Make enough cards so all numerals and shapes are represented.

## #22. "Shape Trace"

*Objectives:*

1. To reinforce recognition of shapes.
2. To reinforce recognition of colors.
3. To develop coordination.

*Procedure:*

On white posterboard cards, about ten by ten inches, draw
a specific shape at the left of each row. Color the shape. To the

right, make some dotted shapes of the exact size and shape as the beginning one. Make less dots on each representation. (See Figure 4-4.) Each row should have a different shape and color. The children then trace over the dotted shapes with the color of the pattern shape. They do not color the shape as it would require too much cleaning, unless, of course, you want them to do so. Make enough cards so all shapes and colors that you will study over the year are represented. This is a good exercise for any time of the year. Laminate your cards for repeated use.

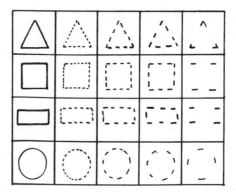

**Figure 4-4**

### #23. "Size and Quantity"

*Objectives for procedures 23-24:*

1. To increase recognition of sets and numerals.
2. To teach meanings of quantitative words.
3. To teach size of sets in relation to other sets.
4. To increase visual discrimination.

*Procedure:*

On a master set make a numeral in the center of the page with sets of different sizes—one to ten—around it. (See Figure 4-5.) You may want to put this on posterboard later and laminate it for permanent use.

There are several things one can do with this paper. Make sure that each child has access to different colored crayons. Then you may ask them to:

1. With a red crayon, circle the sets with the same number of shapes as the numeral.
2. Put a green X on the smallest set.
3. Put a purple (or violet) line through the largest set.
4. Put a yellow line under all the sets that have the same number. These may include those marked in number one.)
5. Put a blue line over the largest set.
6. Put a black line through the set of squares. (Repeat with all colors and shapes.)
7. Use any other size words such as "least," "most," "smallest," "biggest," and so on.
8. The children may work with these independently by circling the ones that represent the numeral. Or, in a group playing "school," the "teacher" may give specific directions as you have done.

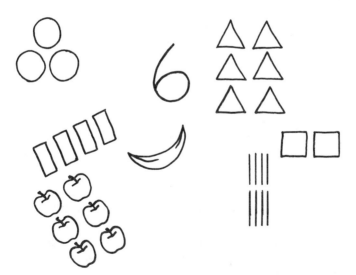

**Figure 4-5**

#24. "Sizing"

*Procedure:*

On a master set (or posterboard that is to be laminated) draw several sets of three or four objects. If you make laminated cards, color your objects to make them more appealing. Even if you start with a master, laminate some for later use. You can always put a copy that has been colored on top of a piece of posterboard of the same size and laminate it.

Since there are many things you can do with this and the previous sheet, making several copies to use on succeeding days with different instructions is advisable. (See Figure 4-6.) Some suggestions for using this sheet are:

1. Look at all the sets and put a red line under the tallest object in each set.
2. Put a green line over the shortest object in each set.
3. In the sets of three objects, put a yellow line through the middle-sized one.
4. In the sets of four objects, find any two objects of the same size and put a brown X on them.
5. Circle the sets of four with a black color.
6. Circle the sets of three with a purple color.
7. Continue with other similar directions.

For Numbers 23 and 24, it is best to divide into smaller groups when possible and have an aide, parent helpers, or older students help you work with small groups to ensure success and to immediately correct any mistakes.

## Learning Math Skills with Classroom Materials.

Many math skills are developed through regular materials found in the classroom. The following are representations of the types of activities in which kindergarteners can engage while learning important math concepts.

**Figure 4-6**

## #25. "Shape Creations"

*Objectives for procedures 25-26:*

1. To develop coordination.
2. To increase knowledge of shapes and how they affect us.
3. To have fun creating pictures.
4. To increase understanding of numeral and set number.

*Procedure:*

During the study of shapes, no doubt you have discussed and observed the many shapes around us. The children have now observed that everything has shape and that most things are made up of very basic shapes. During your art project this week, tell the children that you want them to create any object, animal, or person they want to from the shapes you have cut for them. (Let older students have the honor of cutting circles, squares, triangles, and rectangles of different sizes and colors.)

Show the children several figures that have been created with shapes, then ask them to create their own. They should glue these onto nine- by twelve-inch, or larger, sheets of construction paper. Let them do this each day. At the end of the week, put each child's work in a folder, then let him decorate the outside with shapes and take it home. If you keep the remaining shapes on your art table, the children will use them with other collage materials.

## #26. "See What You Can Create"

*Procedure:*

During the art period on days when each numeral is being introduced, give each child as many objects as the numeral you are studying represents. Ask the children to see what they can create with that many objects. Give each child a sheet of construction paper, have glue available, and tell them that they must decide what scene they can create that includes the objects you gave them.

The objects may be anything: buttons, cotton balls, cupcake liners, pieces of fabric, beans, corn, leaves, etc. For instance, if you give each child four beans, one might draw some flowers and use the beans for centers; another might use them for fruit on their tree. Another might draw a clown and use the beans for buttons. Someone might use them for shoes. Another might draw a brook scene and use the beans as stones on which to cross the brook. The uses are only limited to the imagination of the youngster who is doing the creating.

## #27. "Clay Numerals"

*Objectives:*

1. To have fun with a pliable substance.
2. To reinforce numeral name and set number.
3. To develop coordination.
4. To develop tactile perception.

*Procedure:*

Nearly every child will make numerals out of clay whether he is asked to or not. The reason? They are simply designed characters and easy to make. Spend a day now and then during an art period making clay numerals, or else the children may learn to make them incorrectly—on their own. The feel of the clay, the feel of the numerals as they are traced, and the pride of accomplishment are all worth the time spent. Numerals may be made in two ways:

1. Roll out long thin strips of clay and with short pieces form numerals.
2. Roll out the clay into a flat piece and use a pencil or other object to draw the numeral in the clay.

Have the children put their numerals in ascending order and make matching sets if enough clay is available.

### #28. "Bead Sequence"

*Objectives for procedures 29-30:*

1. To develop sequencing ability.
2. To increase visual perception for color, shape, and order.
3. To increase language skills.

*Procedure:*

You probably have a box of patterns that you bought to go with your stringing beads. If not, I hope you will consider them in the future. In the meantime, you can make your own patterns as you work with the children. A small group of children with an older person is best for this activity. You, or an aide, should make a copy that you want the children to duplicate. For instance, suppose the beads you string are like this: three large blue squares, two small yellow squares, and two large red circular shapes. The children look at yours, duplicate it, and see if they can continue duplicating it to the end of their string. This particular pattern is one of the more difficult ones. To begin these exercises you would have only two differences.

### #29. "Block Stacking"

*Procedure:*

The same approach is used with blocks and the patterns that require specific stacking procedures. The pattern should be made in front of the children in the beginning, but later the children should duplicate the pattern cards. After the children learn how to "read" the pattern cards and can duplicate them, an older student to guide them is all that is necessary.

### #30. "Pegs"

*Procedure:*

Patterns can also be bought with your pegs and pegboards. Again, the children must learn to sequence correctly with the proper number and color. Pegs are one of the smaller materials and require finer motor control than the other two sets of sequential material. In the beginning, make a pattern as the children watch, but later they should be able to "read" the pattern cards.

## Learning Math Skills Through Exciting Games and Art Activities

As in all other areas in which kindergarten children are involved, art activities and games play an important role in the development of math skills. You are encouraged to add similar experiences such as the following to the curriculum.

### #31. "Treasure Hunt"

*Objectives:*

1. To reinforce numeral recognition.
2. To reinforce number of set belonging to a specific numeral.
3. To enjoy a game that will increase math skills.

*Procedure:*

Have an older student or parent helper supervise each group of five children. Make up an illustrated list for each child. (See Figure 4-7.) The child is to "read" his list, then find and bring to the helper the items on the list. When every child in the group has completed his list, the helper goes over each list with the group. They all decide if they found the correct items and the correct number of items. Five different articles on each list are sufficient for an activity period. Take up the lists and give to different children on another day. If you laminate these lists, they can be used for many years. However, you will have to use items on the lists that are always found in kindergarten rooms, if they are to be used in the future.

**Figure 4-7**

#32. "Dear Parents"

*Objectives:*

1. To inform parents of the child's success.
2. To enjoy an art project.
3. To develop coordination.

*Procedure:*

At the end of a month of study on numeral recognition, have a special art project. Make a master and run it off on nine-by twelve-inch white construction paper. On the master write:

Dear Parents,

I know all of my numerals from one through ten.
(Child writes his name here.)

Give each child green paper to make a flower stem, or let him cut out one that you have made on a master copy. They should glue this to the construction paper under the letter and add ten yellow petals that they have cut out. On the petals, the children write all the numerals they have learned. When completed, give the children some brown paper (or other color) and let them cut out a circular shape for the center of the flower. (See Figure 4-8.)

**Figure 4-8**

If some children have not learned all the numerals, they should either leave their flower at school in order to add more petals later, or, add only enough petals to represent the numerals they know. You can then cross out the "one to ten" on the letter and write in the ones they know. Be sure you have made a note of the children who need more help and the ones who do not. The ones who know all the numerals will not have to be tested again. This will save you a lot of time.

### #33. "Merry-Go-Round"

*Objectives:*

1. To reinforce counting to ten.
2. To reinforce recognition of numerals to ten. (You can go further later.)
3. To learn while enjoying a game.

*Procedure:*

For this activity, you should have a group of five or six with a helper. Make a laminated board on which you have written all the numerals. (See Figure 4-9.) Put a spinner in the center of the board. A child spins, and as the spinner stops on a numeral, he tells another child, "You can ride the merry-go-round (spin the next time) if you can count this far." Or, he can say, ". . . if you can show me this many fingers." If that child can do what he is asked, he gets a turn to spin. If he cannot, the same child gets to spin again.

Make boards for colors, shapes, letters (can be used for sounds also), or any other naming symbols. These boards can also be used for testing. The person testing must make notes of those children needing more help.

**Figure 4-9**

Other chapters throughout this book have math activities that you will want to use. Remember to make math an exciting subject!

# 5

## Effective Ways to Promote Language Skills

### Why Language Development Is Our Most Valuable Asset

Without some way to communicate our needs to others, we could not survive. And just as communication affects our survival, so language development, or the lack of it, affects kindergarten children. Our educational systems are geared to the development of the communicative skills of speaking, reading, and writing. This is why it is extremely important in kindergarten to develop a language background that covers every aspect of our environment. As the children are then introduced to the written language in first grade, they are prepared to understand the meaning that the writer is seeking to convey.

Thus, your task is manifold. Besides a background in special skills, language preparation is a must. It cannot be separated from the specific skills, nor is it of any less importance. On the contrary, skills are more easily taught when children understand what is expected and the terms of reference are used.

## Developing Language Skills Through Books

It is through books that children hear being read to them that learning outside of daily occurrences takes place. It is also through the methods in which children are exposed to books that they learn either to like or dislike them. It is important that you make books an exciting and cherished tool through which learning can take place.

### #1. "Reading the Pictures"

*Objectives for procedures 1-2:*

1. To encourage interest in books.
2. To develop sequential skills.
3. To develop understanding of picture detail.
4. To encourage usage of the tape recorder.

*Procedure:*

Most children love to read to their younger siblings. Kindergarten children are no exception. Take advantage of this desire to impart knowledge to others by letting each child select a book that he would like to "read" to himself or to others.

Show the children how to speak into a microphone, how the tape recorder works, and how each child's voice sounds on the recorder by having each child say his name and then replaying it for the class. Let each child then take his book to a quiet corner and "read" the pictures as it is being taped. Some will want you with them, others will not. Some will want another child with them to provide encouragement. Get these reluctant ones started, then step aside, keeping a watchful eye.

Play the story with each child after he records it. Have him point to each picture as he hears it on the recorder. If he does a good job, ask him if you can let the others hear his story too. If so, emphasize all the positive points and skip the negative ones. You want the children to emulate the positive points and not be afraid of negative criticism.

If you have helpers who assist you regularly, let two or three take over the task of recording picture reading once a month with the children. Replay as many as you can to comment on the progress being made.

## #2. "Telling Stories"

*Procedure:*

This activity is similar to the first one, except in this one the children tell a familiar story as it is recorded. If you have enough tapes to store each child's stories for the year on one, do try this. After each story is taped, replayed, and comments on positive points are made to the class, save the tape for the next time. Start the following story at the end of the first, and so on. The parents, you, and the children will all be able to see the progress. Again, it is advisable to have helpers working with the children as they record their stories. These would make excellent Mother's Day gifts to take home near the end of the school year.

## Self-Expression Through Active Experiences

It is through dramatic productions, regardless of how insignificant to us, that children really learn new language skills as they act out their understanding of new stories, poems, songs, etc.

## #3. "Performance Day"

*Objectives for procedures 3-4:*

1. To develop confidence.
2. To encourage participation in group activities.
3. To evaluate past learning situations.
4. To increase language skills.

*Procedure:*

After all of your children have become well acquainted with each other and like to share their experiences with one another (you can tell through "Show and Tell" time), set aside a day once every two weeks or so to let the children perform before the class. They will do this in groups of three or four children—as many as are needed for their particular activity. Our kindergarten children took their free time each Friday to decide on what activity they wanted to perform. And, oh, the secrecy they employed! It was fascinating to watch. Most of them did not even want me to know. Others would tell me in order to get props and materials needed. Shy children should be skillfully maneuvered into groups of extroverts, but this is easily done.

Some will do nursery rhymes, some a story, a puppet show, a song, etc. The entire performance will not take long, but the children will be extremely impressed with themselves.

As the children become more sure of themselves and have upgraded their performances, invite the parents in some day to watch. What the children are actually doing is repeating the things they have been taught in class. It is an excellent way to review and evaluate the learning the children have done.

#### #4. "Puppetry"

*Procedure:*

Retrieve someone's refrigerator box or ask a store to save you one if you do not have something behind which children can perform puppet shows. They can be one of your best avenues for listening and interpretive skills.

Once a month or so, ask everyone to divide into groups to perform a familiar story, nursery rhyme, song, or to make up their own activity. Be sure that the shy ones are placed with outgoing children and that leaders are interspersed among the several groups.

Some mothers or fathers may help make puppets for special

stories. The children may make bag puppets especially for the part they are going to portray in the show. Use whatever you have and add to it each year.

You may have some truly magnificent announcers among your students. If so, let them announce each act and make comments. I have seen a few children who were naturals. They made the show. Everyone was impressed with their performance. In fact, the show was excellent because of them. Again, you may want to invite parents to a show some day.

## Encouraging Creative Attributes

#### #5. "My Own Story"

*Objectives:*

1. To encourage oral expression.
2. To increase sequential ability.
3. To develop a story book made by the students.

*Procedure:*

After children have had experiences telling stories from pictures, let each child tell a story to you, an aide, or parent helper who writes down what and how the child tells the familiar story. This is then typed on a master set under the title and the name of the author. One story on each half page is generally sufficient space at this level.

When all the stories have been mimeographed, cut the pages in half so the storybook is approximately four by five-and-a-half inches. Put covers on the back and let each child illustrate the cover of his book with pictures that represent his story. When completed, the books may be taken home for the parents to read.

#### #6. "Recipes" or "A Jewel to Treasure"

*Objectives:*

1. To make a Mother's Day gift (or for some other occasion).
2. To encourage expression.

3. To encourage creative thinking.

*Procedure:*

We often make this gift for Mother's Day. It is a unique and different gift that any mother or grandmother would treasure. Tell each child that he is going to give his mother his favorite food recipe for her gift. Ask the children to keep it a secret until they take it home. They really think it is special now. Some may say that they do not know how to make something. Tell them that none of the children know exactly how, but they are going to try to remember how their mothers have made it before and tell you what they did. You will have to say from time to time, "And what is next?" or "How much do you think you will need?" If they say "A whole bunch," put that in the recipe. The results are hilarious and very much appreciated.

Type these on master sets, each recipe with the child's name on a half sheet as in the previous activity. Cut in half and put covers on the outside. Mimeograph this poem on the inside of the front cover. Have the children sign their name at the bottom.

> "A special recipe book
> Comes to you today.
> Won't you try my favorite dish,
> And not be too dismayed?
> It may not turn out as you wish,
> But it comes with love on Mother's Day."

## #7. "Poetry"

*Objectives for procedures 7-8:*

1. To develop rhyming ability.
2. To increase auditory perception.
3. To learn new words and ways to use them.

*Procedures:*

Using vocabulary words discussed in your unit studies, make up short poems to which the children respond with the last word. Later, as they become adept, let them fill in the complete last line. If you cannot make up rhymes, use books. Many include poems about almost any subject.

Let us suppose that you are studying about spring. Here is a sample poem to which children can add a word or line:

"The rains come;
The flowers grow.
Let's pick some,
Before we (go)."

Another for fall might read:

"Hear the dry leaves crackly under your feet.
Don't the red, yellow and orange ones look so (sweet, neat)."

### #8. "Speedy"

*Procedure:*

Play this in small groups with helpers. The helper first says a word and the next child says a rhyming word as quickly as he can, and so on, around the circle. As the children mature, quicken the pace. The words can be nonsense words as long as they rhyme. Start with simple words such as game, ball, can, bat, or sit. Increase the word length as children are ready. When a child cannot think of another word, he is out until the next game. The idea is to see who can stay in the longest.

### #9. "Charades"

*Objectives for procedures 9-10:*

1. To develop the ability to speak through actions.
2. To increase sequencing ability.
3. To increase language understanding.

*Procedure:*

With the help of older students or parents, let each small group of children decide on a nursery rhyme, song, finger play, or story that they want to act out for the others. The helpers should encourage the children to act their part in such a way that it will not be too difficult for others to guess. They must also remind the children not to speak, but to use gestures only. At first, the helpers will need to go over the actions with the children, but after some practice, the children will be able to do charades by themselves.

#10. "Picture Talk"

*Procedure:*

Let each child choose a partner. Give each pair a large sheet of paper pre-folded into fourths to depict a nursery rhyme, song, story, or finger play. Remind the children that they must remember what happened first, second, third, and last. Each scene must also follow the next on the four sections of paper. If necessary, show the children where to start and how to proceed on their paper.

When everyone has finished, each pair will show theirs to the others, who must then guess what they have depicted. This is the reason the paper must be large. The others will not be able to see a small picture. You will have some, at first, who will still make theirs small even though you have stressed large scenes. They will see why when they are shown to others.

Start this activity early in the year and continue throughout the year. Eventually, every child will learn to assemble a scene in order of progression if he has been exposed to it enough.

## Special Language Building Aids

The correct noun or pronoun and the verbs used with them are often difficult for young children to learn. The following are some examples of the types of activities that stress this important concept within the structure of complete sentences.

#11. "Say the Whole Thing"

*Objectives:*

1. To develop sentence structure ability,
2. To encourage correct language usage.

3. To provide a background for future language skills.

*Procedure:*

There are some good language programs on the market for kindergarten children. The purpose of any language program should be to provide children with the type of communication skills necessary to correctly transfer the spoken or written language to others. If you do not have a program, begin the first week teaching your children to speak and answer questions in full sentences. For instance, you might ask, "Did you go to the zoo, Jane?" Jane replies, "Yes." To this you say, "Yes, what did you do, Jane?" She answers by saying, "Yes, I went to the zoo."

Saying the "whole thing" or speaking in full sentences provides the child with correct and complete sentence structure from the beginning. It also paves the way for correctly written sentences in later school years.

## #12. "Story Sequence"

*Objectives:*

1. To develop sequencing ability.
2. To increase visual perception.
3. To increase ability to relate one scene to a following one.

*Procedure:*

If you do not have sequential stories that are made similar to puzzle boards, try making some. Find old reading readiness books no longer in use, cut out the pictures of apparent sequential happenings, glue them on squares of posterboard, laminate them, and let the children arrange them in the proper order.

There should be no more than three or four pictures for each story, particularly at the beginning of the year. You can add longer scenes as children mature.

Another source of sequential material is the comic strip section of the newspaper. The only problem with these is that you have to be careful in your selection. Children must be able to work out a sequence without too much difficulty. If they are too difficult, they will not work with them unless forced.

## The Advantages of Nursery Rhymes and Finger Plays

Nursery rhymes and finger plays are used abundantly in kindergarten. Their rhythmic lines are adapted to getting and keeping the attention of little children. The important thing that you should remember is to make the rhymes and plays as active as possible in order to further enhance their effectiveness as teaching tools. Chapter 4 of my previous book gives some specific suggestions for actions and changes for the more common nursery rhymes.

*Objectives for procedures 13-18:*

1. To develop understanding of words.
2. To offer a fun way to improve coordination and language skills.
3. To develop sequencing ability.
4. To develop listening skills.

### #13. "The Crooked Man"

*Procedure:*

This is a sample of the way nursery rhymes can be performed. Let one child be the crooked man. The child attempts to make himself appear crooked. He then starts walking in a zigzag manner. Each time another subject is mentioned, such as the sixpence and the cat and mouse, another child follows the leader about the room. At the end, they all sit down in their "crooked house." If you have suitable furniture, construct a stile in order to provide a visual stimulus for the word.

### #14. "Hush-a-Bye Baby"

*Procedure:*

The children should have a partner for this song. They face each other, hold both hands, and pretend to be rocking a baby as they sway back and forth as if in the wind. When the bough (tell the children that this is a branch) breaks, the children fall to the floor.

### #15. "Diddle Diddle Dumpling"

*Procedure:*

This is a good nursery rhyme to use when you want to help children learn to tie their shoes or to find those who need help with tying. First, have the girls say the poem as it is written while the boys lie on the floor as if in bed. They must have one shoe off. At the end of the rhyme, the boys quickly sit up and tie their shoes as the girls say:

"Tie it fast,
Or tie it slow,
But tie it in a double bow."

When the boys have their shoes on, it is the girls' turn to lie down with one shoe off. Now the boys must change the name to a girl's name and change the pronoun *his* to *her*. For instance, the poem may now sound something like this:

"Diddle diddle dumpling
My girl Rose,
Went to bed with her stockings on.
One shoe off, one shoe on,
Diddle diddle dumpling
My girl Rose."

When the boys have finished, the girls sit up and tie their shoes as quickly as possible while the boys say the "Tie" poem.

## #16. "What Are Boys and Girls Made Of?"

*Procedure:*

Change this song to say:

"What are little boys made of? Made of?
What are little boys made of?
Shirts, pants, shoes and socks,
Caps, coats, balls and tops,
That's what little boys are made of.

"What are little girls made of? Made of?
What are little girls made of?
Dresses, bows, slacks and shirts,
Shoes, socks, dolls and skirts,
That's what little girls are made of."

You may change the items to any other you wish; e.g., items of equipment, utensils, transportation, etc.

## #17. "Two Little Dicky Birds"

*Procedure:*

Change this finger play to say:

"Two Little Dicky birds
Sitting on my hands. (*Hold out both hands.*)
One on Susie; (*Put down one hand, extend other.*)
One on Jan. (*Same as for Susie.*)
Fly away to Tommy; (*Tommy extends one hand.*)
Fly away to Ben. (*Ben extends one hand.*)
Come back to Susie;
Come back to Jan."

For this rhyme, have two children stand in front of two other children. Change the names of the children to those in the group. As Susie is named, she holds out one hand. Jan does likewise. When they fly to the others, the child, Susie, shakes hands with Tommy. Jan shakes hands with Ben. As they come back, the girls bring their hands back to their sides. When the children learn this, all the class may group into fours, all performing it at once.

**#18. "My Nose"**

*Procedure:*

This is an example of how you can make up your own finger plays or rhymes:

"Hands? Toes?
Pigeons? Rose?
What's that sitting on my nose?
Well, Well!
Do tell!
Three little freckles on little Nell!"

## Help from Kindergarteners in Improving Home-School Relationships

The more communication you have with parents concerning the activities in which their children are involved in school, the greater support, understanding, and faith they will have in you as a teacher.

**#19. "The Kindergarten Press"**

*Objectives:*

1. To develop abilities to relate happenings correctly.
2. To develop a newsletter for parents.
3. To develop speaking ability.

*Procedure:*

Tell the children at the beginning of school that they are going to be the reporters for a parent newsletter. Their job is to remember the things they did in school and relate them to you. At the end of each day, let each child tell something that was done or learned that day. Take notes of the children's ideas. At the end of the month, compile all the happenings into a newsletter. Add any special notes you have for the parents and occasionally add a short personal note about each child.

Parents appreciate these letters more than anyone could imagine. Also, be sure to send copies to school administrators.

They will be extremely impressed with the busy kindergarten class.

## Games That Will Improve Language Skills

#20. "Picture Bingo"

*Objectives for procedures 20-23:*

1. To promote language skills through object recognition.
2. To increase visual and auditory perception.
3. To encourage participation through games.

*Additional objectives for procedure 23:*

4. To recognize the importance of speaking clearly and carefully.
5. To emphasize the need for listening carefully.

*Procedure:*

In order to teach children to recognize many different objects, cut out all kinds of pictures from books in which you can find at least four or more of the same object. They do not have to be exactly alike as long as they are the same object. Find as many unusual items as you can in order to increase vocabulary and understanding. Paste the pictures on Bingo cards and laminate them. Let a small group of children play the game with a helper. The caller's part should be written on blank playing cards for ease in shuffling. These cards will have the names of the objects on them. For instance, there might be a bed, lawn mower, hay baler, etc.

You can use these same Bingo cards to play rhyming Bingo games. For instance, the helper draws a card with "bed" written on it. He/She says, "Cover the picture that rhymes with 'red.'" Nonsense words can be made up for the more difficult words. For helpers who might not be able to think of words to rhyme with the pictures, write several words that rhyme on the card with the name of the object. If the name is written in one color of ink and the rhyming words in another, it will be less confusing.

## #21. "Match-Up"

*Procedure:*

Draw or glue pictures of different items on blank playing cards. Laminate the cards in order to keep the picture intact. The children play this as they would "Memory."™ They turn over two cards at each turn, trying to get two that are alike. The one with the most sets wins.

If you select pictures that rhyme, some of the "Match-Up" games can be played by having the children turn up two cards with pictures of rhyming words.

## #22. "Books"

*Procedure:*

Use the same cards used for the "Match-Up" games above and let the children play "Books," in which they call for matching pictures from others. If they are playing with the rhyming cards, they must ask for a picture that rhymes with one they have. The winner is the one who has the most sets of two cards.

## #23. "Gossip"

*Procedure:*

Everyone knows how to play "Gossip." One person whispers a sentence to another and it is repeated around the circle. If you have several helpers, allow six children to each helper who directs the game. This is a good game to play before giving puppet shows or performances, as the children will be able to see the need for speaking distinctly.

Many other ideas for developing language skills are in the other chapters. In fact, almost every area of learning in kindergarten must develop language skills relating to that subject before one can proceed from one thought to another. The power of language cannot be overemphasized.

# 6

## Stimulating Kindergarten Experiences Through Exhilarating Musical Adventures

### Why Music Is the Universal Language

Through music every nation in the world can communicate, because everyone understands and enjoys some form of music. Kindergarteners are no exception. On the contrary, most kindergarten-aged children are not yet inhibited by what someone considers to be the right or wrong way of producing rhythmic responses to the sounds of music.

It is for this reason that music is one of the best and most exciting avenues through which kindergarteners can learn all skills. With the exceptional recordings on the market today, almost any skill can be magnified through the wonderfully exhilarating field of music.

### Enjoy Music and Games as You Develop Coordination

*Objectives for procedures 1-6:*

1. To develop coordination.
2. To enjoy music and games.

3. To develop listening and interpretative skills.

### #1. "Balloon Beat"

*Procedure:*

This activity might be part of a party or holiday celebration. Give each child a balloon. Let each blow up his balloon and with helpers tie the balloons so they do not leak air.

Use a recording with a simple walk beat. Tell the children that they are to keep their balloons in the air by batting them in time to the music. As the children learn to do the walk beat, change to a different beat with a faster pace and, finally, to an uneven beat.

### #2. "Ball Beat"

*Procedure:*

Using the same procedure as in the previous activity, let the children keep time with the music while dribbling a nine-inch ball. Each child has his own ball, and if he cannot dribble it, he may bounce it in time with the music. If this activity is used during the last half of the year, most children should be able to do a fair job of dribbling. Encourage a continuous dribbling action.

Start with slow walking beats and over a period of time introduce faster and uneven beats. Or, the children may dribble on the strong beats, every other beat, every fourth beat, etc. This activity requires mature listening skills which will not be evidenced in some children by this time.

### #3. "Hot Ball"

*Procedure:*

Play this as you would play "Hot Potato" and "Musical Chairs" combined. The object is to pass the ball as quickly as possible from one person to the next. However, in this musical game, the addition of music that stops suddenly, adds excitment to the game. The person with the ball when the music stops is out of the game. Play until only one child is left.

## #4. "Animal Trap"

*Procedure:*

Make traps of jump ropes or hula hoops and place them around the room. Arrange these in such a manner that the children must go from one to the other and must move continually. Each child must also go through every trap. If he skips one, he is out of the game.

As the music plays, children move in a manner specified before the game starts. You may want them to skip, hop on one foot, crawl, leap, etc. When the music stops, those inside the traps are "caught" and are out of the game. The last one remaining without getting trapped is the winner.

## #5. "Musical Charades"

*Procedure:*

After your children have learned how charades are done, let them try characterizations to music. This activity should start with the entire group performing simple charades in time to music. As the children learn the procedure, the groups may be divided into smaller ones with an aide or parent helper supervising each group.

The children may wish to portray an animal or vehicle in motion, they may pretend to be playing a musical instrument or to be going on a trip, or they may wish to try a nursery rhyme or short story. You will have to provide a suitable musical selection that will heighten the dramatization.

## #6. "Musical Mirror Images"

*Procedure:*

Let each child choose a partner for this activity. Or, you may wish to arrange less rhythmic children with those who perform well. One child pretends he is standing before a mirror while the other one is the image who must imitate the leader. As the music plays—start with something slow, such as swaying movements—the leader starts his movement with his partner attempting to duplicate him in every respect. The partner should become the leader after a few minutes.

Do these mirroring activities often, particularly when you have students who need to develop a rhythmic sense for certain musical selections.

### #7. "Musical Instruments"

*Objectives:*

1. To develop listening and interpretative skills.
2. To develop rhythmic skills.
3. To encourage participation and to have fun.
4. To increase musical pleasure.

*Procedure:*

It is not necessary that you buy musical instruments, but at least one set of rhythm instruments is good to have. Drums and rhythm sticks can be made. Whatever you use, children should have the opportunity to use them often.

When beginning with rhythm instruments, start with simple and rather slow movements. Increase the tempo and add more complicated rhythms as the children increase in ability.

After the children have learned to keep time to musical selections, let them move in time to the music while keeping time on the instruments at the same time. This is difficult for some children to do. They attempt to do both, but soon they are concentrating on only one aspect of the rhythmical process. Some of the following activities, along with others, may be done in time to rhythmic selections. For the following, the children should be divided into pairs, or they may be divided in such a way that half of the children face the other half in two lines.

1. One half beats the drums while the other half dribbles the ball. (Both on the same beat.)

2. One half uses rhythm sticks as the other half jumps rope. The children with rhythm sticks hit them together as the ropes touch the floor. The children watch only one child for this. Later, they hit the sticks when the rope hits the floor and as it goes over the jumping child's head.

3. One half puts a bell loop on each wrist and keeps time with the others as they keep time with a hula hoop.

4. Add all the combinations you wish.

## How to Produce Musical Selections to Accommodate Your Special Needs

#8. "Recording Music"

*Objectives:*

1. To offer an alternative to unrecorded selections.
2. To allow the teacher to always be with the children during musical procedures.
3. To add to the collection of possibilities for future use.

*Procedure:*

Even if you play a musical instrument, musical activities should always be performed while you are with the children. They need you, and you need to be sure that they understand and perform correctly, particularly when a basic skill is involved.

What if you have a selection to play—this is often the case when using guide books—and you need the music that is not recorded? Record your own music for the selection ahead of time. Play it over and over to the end of the tape, with short pauses inbetween. This allows you to play it several times without having to stop to rewind.

Label the selection according to number, name, and unit

and make a file card with the same information plus the words to the music. When the selection is needed, look in your file box and you can readily see which tape you need to get. On the opposite side of the tape and card, put the same type of information about the music on that side. To the right of your selection title, write the name of the selection on the other side. At a glance you are able to see the title for both sides regardless of which side faces you. Tapes file very neatly with the cards in a three- by five-inch file box. There is no need to separate the cards and tapes unless you just want to.

Perhaps you are, as many of us are, unable to play your own selections. There may be someone who would volunteer to do it, perhaps a parent. Or, you may exchange work with a music teacher who can do it for you. Or, you may do as I have done, rely on other recordings. Sometimes there are similar musical selections on other recordings.

## The Aesthetic Enjoyment Gained Through Combinations of Art and Music

#9. "Artistic Rhythms"

*Objectives:*

1. To enjoy an art project to the rhythm of music.
2. To develop coordination.
3. To develop rhythm.
4. To develop listening and interpretative skills.

*Procedure:*

Give each child a large sheet of butcher paper and some crayons. Play a slow rhythmic recording and tell the children to make the motion that the music suggests. In order for the children to understand the process, you should be working on a large sheet of paper at the front of the room.

Increase the tempo and add rhythms for skipping, jumping, hopping, running, etc. Ask the children to try to "feel" the rhythms as they move their crayons about.

At a later date, let the children use paint with brushes, finger paints, etc., with the same types of rhythmic selections. The children can enjoy both the music and the art activities; therefore, combinations will be doubly satisfying.

## Using Recordings to Foster Exciting Learning Experiences

Although I would ordinarily not send you outside this book for material with which to work, the wonderful and exciting recordings by Hap Palmer are something of which I want every kindergarten teacher to be aware. I have talked with many kindergarten teachers and, without exception, the one thing they would not want to be without were these recordings. Their cost is nominal and the excitement and learning they generate can be compared to no other teaching tool. I personally recommend them as the most dynamic materials that you can add to your teaching supplies.

The address of one company from which you may order them is *Educational Activities, Inc.,* Box 392, Freeport, New York 11520. They have other recordings that are good for kindergarten also. One is *Dancing Numerals,* an album by Henry Glass, Rosemary Hallum, et al.

All of Hap Palmer's recordings—though not all are for kindergarteners—are filled with the excitement of learning that every teacher hopes to achieve. Another factor that contributes to their phenomenal success is that children are required to be actively involved in the learning. Children never forget when they can learn through such exciting experiences.

Some of these recordings are used in daily lesson arrangements in the following activities. The lessons include coordination activities, social and emotional attributes, language skills needed for basic skills, and special subject matter.

## Examples of Activities That Can Be Derived from Recorded Music

### Five Sample Lessons for the First Quarter

*Objectives for all the following lessons:*

1. To reinforce the shapes of a circle, triangle, and square.
2. To reinforce color recognition.
3. To develop language skills.
4. To develop coordination skills.
5. To increase listening and interpretative skills.
6. To reinforce safety rules.
7. To develop understanding of emotions.
8. To develop visual and tactile skills.

#### #10. "The Circle" (Hap Palmer)

*Procedure:*

Use your regular home bases marked with hula hoops or jump ropes folded in a circle. Each child stands outside his circle and performs actions as he sings to the recording.

As a follow-up, give each child a dittoed sheet of paper on which you have drawn several circles. With a crayon, have the children mark the circle as you give directions. Give similar directions to those on the recording. For instance, "With your red crayon, make a mark inside a circle."

#### #11. "Colors" (Hap Palmer)

*Procedure:*

As you teach the colors at the beginning of school, this song reinforces the colors of blue, red, green, and yellow. The delightful words and activities require the children to listen with all diligence.

Cut out large circles of colors and tape them on separate chairs or large blocks. Divide the children into four groups, with a different group standing behind the object on which their color is located. As the song asks a specific color to perform, only that group may execute that action.

As a follow-up, let the children paint with the colors indicated. Those without easels may use watercolors at the tables.

### #12. "Stop, Look and Listen" (Hap Palmer)

*Procedure:*

Play this recording to reinforce the safe way to cross a street. A pretend street made of strips of tape with a corner and a stop sign, if available, are valuable aids in teaching the proper way to cross. You will also be able to emphasize what the word "jaywalking" means.

You will probably want to use this recording often at the beginning of school and occasionally throughout the year as a reminder. Follow up the recording with an art activity. On a master set draw the outline of a traffic signal. Let the children cut out circles of red, yellow, and green to paste on the signal.

### #13. "Feelings" (Hap Palmer)

*Procedure:*

As this is first played, have all the children portray all the emotions on the recording. Later, divide into groups, one group for each emotion. This encourages better listening habits as the children cannot turn to others every time to see what they are doing.

As a follow-up, let the children in each group draw pictures of someone with the emotional expression that they portrayed.

### #14. "Moving Game" (Hap Palmer)

*Procedure:*

This is an excellent recording to use in a daily musical lesson for coordination development. Since this is a pretend song, the children are free to develop their own style of expression.

When the children understand this selection, let them select partners and play the "mirror" game. Each partner should be given an opportunity to be the leader.

## Five Sample Lessons for the Second Quarter

### #15. "How Many Ways" (Hap Palmer)

*Procedure:*

This is another recording that reinforces the concept of triangles, circles, and squares, but with the figure eight added. Have large samples of these written and arranged in front of the children. When they are to draw them in the air, trace around them on your examples. This is particularly important when making the figure eight, as the children probably have not learned how to make it correctly.

As a follow-up, give each child a large sheet of paper on which you have drawn a large figure eight with a black felt-tipped marking pen. Let each child trace around a copy of a circle, triangle, and square, cut them out, and glue them onto the figure eight in such a way that a character is made. It may be a person, animal, vehicle, etc. Let them decide if they want to use all the shapes on their character or if they want to draw other pictures around it using the shapes on the other objects.

### #16. "Brush Away" (Hap Palmer)

*Procedure:*

This is a recording that should be stressed throughout the year. Be sure that the children express the proper procedures for brushing their teeth. If you have a brush and a model set of teeth, use it in front of the children as the words suggest.

Perhaps this is the day you could get a dentist to come to school and demonstrate to the children the proper way to brush their teeth. If not, many dentists' wives take this on as a project. It would be worth a try to see if you could get a "special" someone, since the effect of a representative from the dentist's office is much more profound than the teacher's demonstration.

#17. "Rag Doll" (Hap Palmer)

*Procedure:*

On the day before you are going to play this record for the first time, tell all the girls, and boys, to bring their rag dolls to school if they have one. Show the children the differences between the rag doll and other dolls by comparing them.

After the musical selection has been completed with all the directions for portraying rag dolls carried out, have the children draw a rag doll. See how many display the limp characteristics.

#18. "Elephant Song" (Henry Glass, et al.)

*Procedure:*

This involves counting by adding one more each time. You can either appoint children or, better still, have large numerals written on nine- by twelve-inch construction paper. Pin these on the front of ten children. The other children will be able to see the symbol for the number called. The children may either perform to the rhythm in their own way or they can follow child Number One and reproduce his actions as in the game of "Follow the Leader."

After the lesson, give each group of four or five children a large sheet of butcher paper. As a group effort, the children draw ten elephants, each following the other by holding the tail of the one in front of him. Some children may want to draw their elephants doing tricks.

#19. "Colored Ribbons" (Hap Palmer)

*Procedure:*

Give each child at least four pieces of yarn, each about twelve inches long and of different colors. Each child should choose a partner, although one is not needed for all parts of the selection.

This recording may be used for practice in tying bows and for reviewing colors.

After the music period, let each child choose one piece of yarn he would like to have. The others should be put away for future use. Tell the children to tie their yarn into a double bow. Next, give each child a twelve- by eighteen-inch piece of construction paper. Ask the children to draw a large child. When the drawing is complete, they glue or tape their yarn onto the figure's hair or clothes for a bow.

## Five Sample Lessons for the Third Quarter

### #20. "Growing" (Hap Palmer)

*Procedure:*

This is a health and science lesson on growing or body image. Start with each child on home base, and let each move out from their base and return with each direction change. Use this recording before or during any planting activities.

Following the music lesson, ask the children to draw a picture of a baby and several growth changes. Finally, they will draw an adult. On the back side of this paper, have the children glue a seed. Pumpkin and cucumber seeds are appropriate for this, as they are flat. The children now should draw different stages of the seed as it sprouts and grows into a full-grown plant.

### #21. "Copycats" (Henry Glass, et al.)

*Procedure:*

Before this recording is played, pin large numerals on the children. In order to include every child, more than one child may represent each numeral. The children perform only those activities related to their particular number while they repeat the words after the teacher.

Another way to portray this selection is to line up the children, one half facing the other half. One group chants the leader's part while the other group repeats it. Let each group try both parts. During this portrayal, all the children perform all the actions.

#### #22. "Grandpa Builds a Table" (Hap Palmer)

*Procedure:*

As the children sing, they perform the actions as suggested by the tools in the song. Another method of performing this selection is to divide the children into as many groups as there are tools, and have the members of each group perform "their" tool.

If the tools are available, show them to the children before the music period and indicate how they work. If you have rhythm instruments, let the children decide which instrument best simulates each tool.

When the period is over, give each child a piece of paper and let him draw the tool he portrayed and the instrument, if any, that was used for each one. If the children wish, they may draw other tools around the specified tool.

#### #23. "Cover Your Mouth" (Hap Palmer)

*Procedure:*

Before and during the season for colds, review this recording often to remind children of this sanitary habit. A colorful bulletin board display with people following the rules of the song also would act as a reminder.

As a follow-up, give each child a large sheet of construction paper and ask him to draw a picture of a child who has a cold. When this is complete, give each child a tissue and help each one staple it over the nose and mouth of the figure. Display some of these to encourage children to always use tissues when needed.

#### #24. "Lucky Numbers" (Hap Palmer)

*Procedure:*

On nine-by twelve-inch construction paper, write large numerals from one to twenty, with one numeral on each sheet.

If you have more children, duplicate the numerals. Have all the children make a circle, and place a numeral on the floor in front of each child. Appoint one child to be in the center of the circle. Tell the children not to step on the numerals as they can be used the next time this selection is played.

As the recording starts, the children are marching around the circle of printed symbols. When they hear the bell, they must all stop behind a numeral. Point to each child as quickly as possible and let each tell his numeral name. If a child does not know, tell him and move on. The child in the center now has a turn. He is to close his eyes and turn around in a circle. Upon stopping, the one to whom he is pointing has the lucky number. This person now takes a turn in the center.

## Five Sample Lessons for the Last Quarter

### #25. "Marching Around the Alphabet" (Hap Palmer)

*Procedure:*

Use the same procedure as the preceding activity, except write letters on the cards. Put the letters on both sides, as the children must pick up the letter. As the song stops and you point to the children, they respond with their letter name. Again, if they do not know, tell them and move on quickly. This game should be repeated often during the last quarter, when more stress is being put on learning the letters, either by name or by sound. If you want to use only sounds, have the children respond in this selection with the sounds rather than the names.

### #26. "Left and Right" (Hap Palmer)

*Procedure:*

Place a band on the children's wrists to indicate the left-right difference. Let each child stand in his home base area to begin this activity. As the children move from one activity to the next, they return to the home base.

All the selections on these albums requiring the use of left and right should be used over and over, as this is a difficult concept to teach.

## #27. "Circle Game" (Hap Palmer)

*Procedure:*

Use the home base area as in the preceding activity. Each base is to be identified with either a hula hoop or a jump rope that has been formed into a circle. Remind the children to listen carefully so they can perform all the activities. Parent helpers placed at strategic points can check to see that all are performing correctly.

## #28. "Jack Be Nimble" (Henry Glass, et al.)

*Procedure:*

Use the home base area and let the children jump into and out of a hula hoop or a rope that forms a circle as they count jumps. Again, parent helpers would be advisable for this activity. It is not easy for some children to count and perform at the same time.

After the lesson, ask the children to draw a large figure of Jack jumping over an object of some sort. The object can be anything, but, of course, many will draw a candle.

## #29. "The Monsters" (Henry Glass, et al.)

*Procedure:*

Once you play this recording, get ready to play it again and again. The children are fascinated with these creatures. Although the counting is too advanced for this age group, they will do the counting just to hear the recording, and learn from it. On a large sheet, write all the counting activities they will be doing. As they are to count with the selection, point to the numerals so the children can follow along. You will be surprised at how well they can count these difficult numbers.

After the music lesson, give the children a large sheet of

paper and tell them that you would like to know what these monsters look like. Tell them to draw the monsters as they think they look. Be sure to remark about creative thinking on the part of the students. After all, that is what learning is all about.

**#30. "Skip"** (Henry Glass, et al.)

*Procedure:*

This is actually an addition song. If you can get some candy sticks, do so, or use lollipops. As the song is progressing, hold up the amount it calls out and let the children see how you then put two such amounts together to get the answer. There is no need to use any other math terms than those used on the recording. The important task at this point is to show children the processes involved.

The next time you use this recording, have all the children seated at tables with several small articles in front of them. Instead of skipping, they can keep time by clapping, tapping, etc. When amounts of candy are called, the children pick up that number of objects, put them together with the next amount, and call out the answer on the pause, before the singer can.

## Using Music to Encourage Correct Numeral and Letter Writing

**#31. "Drawing Numerals"** (Henry Glass, et al.)

*Objectives for 31-32:*

1. To learn the proper method to make each numeral and letter.
2. To develop large muscle coordination.
3. To develop a relationship between the name and the method of making each.

*Procedure:*

Use the recording, "Drawing Numerals," from the album, *Dancing Numerals.* Stand in front of the children with your back to them. As they are to draw a numeral in the air, you are to trace over a model you have written on a large sheet of paper. This will allow them to follow a correct example. Place all left-handed children to your right so they will use their left hand for drawing.

#### #32. "Drawing Letters"

*Procedure:*

Although I do not know of a recording that asks students to trace letters in the air, you may record, or have someone do it for you, the following tune to which each letter can be sung. With your back to the children, trace over each letter as they model yours in the air. You may have to alter the tune somewhat for some letters. For the letter *a*, you might sing:

"We go all the way 'round, and then come down,
To make the letter *a*. To make the letter *a*,
To make the letter *a*.
We go all the way 'round, and then come down,
To make the letter *a*."

**Figure 6-1**

For the other letters you may use these:

*b.* "We come straight down and then around"
  ("to make the letter *b*," etc.)

*c.* We curve around, we curve around. . .

*d.* We come straight down, put a hump at the back . . .

*e.* We go straight over and then curve around . . .

*f.* We make a cane and then a bar . . .

*g.* We curve all the way 'round and come way down . . .

*h.* We come straight down, curve out and down . . .

*i.* We come straight down and make a dot . . .

*j.* An upside down cane and than a dot . . .

*k.* We come straight down, make an arm and a leg . . .

*l.* We come straight down, we come straight down . . .

*m.* We come straight down and curve down two times . . .

*n.* We come straight down and curve down one time . . .

*o.* We curve all the way 'round, all the way 'round . . .

*p.* We come way down and curve around . . .

*q.* We come way down and curve in back . . .

*r.* We come straight down and make an arm . . .

*s.* We curve around and around again . . .

*t.* We come straight down and cross over . . .

*u.* We come down, curve up and straight down . . .

*v.* We slant down and then slant up . . .

*w.* We slant down and up, down and up . . .

*x.* We slant down and make a slant across . . .

*y.* We slant way down and slant to join . . .

*z.* We go straight over, slant back, and straight again . . .

There are many other recordings on the same albums with those mentioned in this chapter that are equally as good and as applicable to the kindergarten curriculum. There are also many other good recordings that you can buy. (Less you get the idea that I believe contrariwise.) The reason these particular recordings are mentioned is that they contribute in several ways to developing the many skills we are interested in at the kindergarten level. Most recordings have only one or two such attributes at the most.

All music is fun. It makes us feel young all over again! Enjoy it!

# 7

## Art: The Axis Around Which Kindergarten Development Revolves

### The Immeasurable Realm of Art in Kindergarten

Art is the chief source from which tasks to develop eye-hand coordination in kindergarten classrooms are derived. Our primary purposes for using art in kindergarten are to develop coordination while stimulating uninhibited responses to specific tasks and to have an enjoyable time doing so.

A creative endeavor requires personal involvement, since it is an expression of how we visualize our environment and how we feel about ourselves in relation to it.

Like music, art expression does not need written words to convey a message. It is capable of being understood in any culture.

### Incorporating Simple Shapes in Art Activities

*Objectives for procedures 1-7:*

1. To develop coordination.

2. To encourage creativity.

3. To develop an appreciation for creative productions.

4. To obtain a final item that is lovely to its maker.

5. To develop a better understanding of the language skills necessary for kindergarten.

### #1. "Shape Art"

*Procedure:*

Let older students cut out many shapes of different colored construction paper. The more shapes you have, the better. Those that are left from this project can be used in others or by the individual student who wishes to experiment on his own.

On each table put several of all the shapes cut out. Add to these shapes as you study different ones. Tell the children that they must build a character or object from these shapes. Give them some ideas from your samples, but also give them some ideas of how they might change or improve them. (See Figure 7-1 for some examples.)

**Figure 7-1**

### #2. "Spray Painting"

*Procedure:*

For this activity, the same shapes that were cut for the previous project may be used, or, let the children cut their own and arrange them in some design over a sheet of white construction paper. Show the children how to weigh down their shapes by using small rocks that have been collected for this purpose. Keep the rocks in a container for other spray paintings. The children can easily wash them while playing "house," and they will be ready for use when needed.

In a spray bottle, pour a thin solution of tempera paint. The paint should be poured through a strainer before it is put in the bottle, as it could clog the small hole. By setting a small strainer over a small funnel in your spray bottle, this task will not be difficult.

Let the children spray lightly over their shape design. (Be sure you have a good sprayer on the bottle.) When the paint has dried (it will not take long), the children should pick up their shapes to discover the designs left underneath. The shapes may still be used for other activities, as the paint will not hurt them.


#3. "Can-Top Prints"

*Procedure:*

There are all sorts of gadgets one can use to make prints on paper or cloth without having to make the shapes. Collect all sizes of juice cans, spray-can tops, bottle caps, small plastic boxes of the rectangular or square shapes, cookie cutters, tissue rolls, and so on. These can all be dipped lightly in paint, and prints can be made on paper in any design.

Give the children large sheets of paper for this, particularly if it is their first time, and let them experiment with making designs of their choosing. Later, give a group of children a large piece of butcher paper that will cover part of a bulletin board and let the little printers print to their hearts' content. Give other groups the paper that will complete a bulletin board cover. Use shapes that will represent the time of the year or the current unit of study. For instance, if you are studying animals, animal cookie cutters can be used. Cover your bulletin boards with this paper as a background for your displays.

This type of printing also makes pretty wrapping paper. If you have tissue paper, give each child a sheet to print a design to represent the occasion. If you do not want to use tissue paper, use butcher paper. Although it is heavier, it is also sturdier.

This printing looks very pretty on book covers—fast, but very simple and colorful.

### #4. "One-Shape Object"

*Procedure:*

Before the children come together for the art project, glue one shape in the middle of a sheet of construction paper. You do not have to put the same shape on every sheet. Use older students to help you cut and glue them.

Tell the students that they have been working with shapes for some time, and that now you want them to create one object from the one shape on their construction paper. They may add any features they wish, but the central character or object must have the shape incorporated within it. They should come up with some good ideas by now. Put some of these on the bulletin board covered with shape prints.

### #5. "Finger Prints"

*Procedure:*

After this project has been introduced, you will probably see these prints every time the children get around paint. They are easily done, no one can really goof, and they are cute.

With low, shallow dishes of tempera paint on each table, show the children how to place the ball of their finger into the paint and then make a print on paper. They should practice this several times to learn just how much paint is necessary and the best technique for making good prints.

On a clean sheet of paper have the children make about six prints. Put each child's name on his paper and let it dry. The following day, show the children how to make characters using the finger prints as the body. (See Figure 7-2 for examples.)

These can be made to represent special times of the year or for special occasions. For instance, birds flying south or north in the fall or spring, owls at Halloween, people during a unit on the family. Dad can be the thumb, baby the little finger, etc. Flowers in spring, rocks across brooks, or buttons on clothes are only a few possibilities.

**Figure 7-2**

#### #6. "Shape Scribble"

*Procedure:*

You have all had your children make scribble designs on paper by drawing dark lines in any pattern and filling in the spaces with other colors. For this exercise, we are using shapes. The shape will depend upon what you are teaching at the moment. They may be geometrical shapes, flowers, trees for fall or Christmas, pumpkins for Halloween, turkeys for Thanksgiving, hearts for Valentine's Day, etc. (See Figure 7-3.)

The children first trace the object with felt markers from a stencil on white construction paper. Next, let them use the felt markers to draw a scribble design within the object. The amount of lines and the color used will depend upon what the object is and for what it will be used. The children now color in all the blank spaces between the lines with colors representing the purpose. For instance, if they are working on fall leaves, they can use a brown marking pen for the outline and fill in with red, orange, and yellow. As a change, let the children use water colors occasionally to fill in the blank spaces.

When the object is completed, the children carefully cut it out, leaving the outside lines on the object. These shapes can be used on bulletin boards as borders and as fillers for larger ob-

jects. They make bulletin boards look very lovely and colorful.
They may also be used for other purposes. For instance, a valentine in February can be glued to a card and taken home to parents. They make lovely cards.

**Figure 7-3**

#### #7. "Tissue Paper Background"

*Procedure:*

Tissue paper makes some of the most beautiful articles you
will find anywhere. All kindergarteners can learn to work with
it, and the outcome is lovely.

For this project, you will need a piece of tagboard or
cardboard for each child. Any size is suitable. Cut out circles of
tissue paper. The colors will depend upon their use. Tell the
children to dab a small paint brush into a mixture of glue and
water and lightly dab this to the center of each circle. If they use
too much glue, the outcome will be a plastered-down look. As
they glue each piece onto the tagboard, they should lap one over
the other until the entire board is covered. Some children may
spread the pieces out and leave spots. Insist that they complete
the assignment by covering every spot. Children must learn to
do things properly.

When the cards are covered, lay them aside to dry. Before
you leave to go home, stack them together and put something
heavy on them if you are using tagboard, or they will curl; a
heavier paper will not.

The following day, the children will add objects to their
cards. The objects will depend upon what is being studied. They

may glue fall leaves that have been gathered and pressed between pages, seeds that they have gathered or brought from home, shapes that have scribbled designs on them, buttons, designs cut from cloth, or other odds and ends. Any substance that is used should be organized in a neat and orderly design.

The children may also cover large shapes of people, animals, fowls, food, holiday items, etc. After they are covered, the children can add beans, corn, buttons, seeds, etc., to make facial features and other needed apparatus.

## Using Nature's Abundance to Amplify Science Studies

Just working with things gathered in our surroundings teaches children many concepts that would otherwise be too difficult for them to understand at this age. Work with nature and it will work for you.

*Objectives for procedures 8-16:*

1. To develop a background of science and nature concepts.
2. To increase pleasure derived from learning about nature.
3. To increase vocabulary.
4. To develop coordination.
5. To encourage creativity.

### #8. "Collection Day"

*Procedure:*

In the fall when the leaves of all colors are falling is the time one can develop interesting and lovely art projects for kindergarten children. Seeds and wild flowers are also abundant at this season and can be used in similar projects.

Before working on any project, have a collection day. If you have trees and plants around the school, let the children collect all the pretty leaves and flowers they can find. If not, and this is generally the case, tell the children to collect these at home.

Give this assignment on a weekend, as some children may be going to other places from which they can bring some different and interesting specimens. Send a short note to the parents telling them of your assignment and they will help too.

Following the collection day, give each child an old magazine and let him place his specimen between the pages for pressing. Afterwards, put a weight on the magazines. After a week or so, the plants may be used for all the art projects you have in mind.

### #9. "Leaf People"

*Procedure:*

Let each child select a large leaf from his magazine. Staple each leaf to a nine- by twelve-inch sheet of construction paper. The children now add the head, arms, legs, feet, etc., to complete the leaf person. These can be put on a yellow, orange, or red background and put on a bulletin board for display.

To make a leaf family, several leaves may be used, some smaller than others. These, too, are stapled to paper and the features added. If the children want, they may add a house around their characters or a landscape for an outside scene.

### #10. "Special Characters"

*Procedure:*

The children will need leaves or plants according to the subject they choose in this project. For instance, suppose the children are making a witch on a broom. One leaf is her body, as in the previous exercise. When the form has been completed, the broom may be added. The children may select a flower or other plant that branches out for the broom. This is also stapled where the children indicate.

A child pulling a wagon loaded with leaves during fall clean-up time can be made with a leaf for the child's body and several tiny leaves to fill the wagon. The child's features are drawn in, as are those of the wagon.

#11. "Birds and Animals"

*Procedure:*

During the study of the fall season or Halloween and Thanksgiving, the possibilities are abundant for using leaves, seeds, and plants.

Add to the witches some bats and owls. For the owl, an oval leaf is perfect, while a bat needs a small oval leaf for a body with smaller leaves for the wings. The wings will need several leaves layered under the body leaf. The children should be able to glue these to construction paper. If you see that the leaves are coming off, you can staple them. When the features are added to these animals, some of them can be added to the bulletin board display of witches.

Birds flying south can be added to a fall scene by stapling a few willow leaves to the sky area. The features are then added to finish the birds.

To make a Halloween night scene, the children can make small bats and owls flying through the air, a witch on her broomstick, shocks of corn made of plants, and a fence made with small willow leaves for posts, connected with felt marker or crayon drawings.

To make a turkey, the children can make a body out of their hand, with the thumb as the head. The tail is usually made of the fingers, but this time, leaves will be glued on over the fingers to make the turkey's tail.

For a lovely pheasant, the children should draw the head and front part of the body. Then long leaves, such as willow, can be glued on. The tail may be made as long as the children wish. Do not be surprised if some tails trail across the page.

#12. "Leaf Prints"

*Procedure:*

Let the children select three or four leaves. They should lay these on an old newspaper or other substance to keep the table clean. Using fall colors of paint, they now cover one side of each leaf with the paint. If this has not been done already, the leaves should now be placed in a neat design that will fit a large sheet of construction paper. Taking a clean white sheet of construction paper, they lay it carefully over their arrangement, pressing the paper down carefully and rubbing it gently to take up the paint from the leaves. The paper is turned over and the leaves carefully removed. When the paint has dried, the prints make lovely additions to fall bulletin board scenes. Or, the children may trace around the edges of the leaves with a contrasting felt-tipped marking pen and cut out the leaves as fillers for larger scenes on the bulletin boards. Cutting should be attempted only around smooth-edged leaves.

### #13. "Spatter Leaf Prints"

*Procedure:*

This procedure is similar to the preceding one except the children arrange their leaves on top of a sheet of white construction paper. The leaves should now be weighted down by the small rocks gathered for this purpose. Using a spray bottle in which thin tempera paint has been poured, the paper around the leaves is carefully sprayed. When the leaves are removed, the white shape of a leaf is revealed. If these are now traced around with a contrasting-color, felt-tipped marking pen, they can be used for bulletin boards, book covers, or a number of other things. Each child can be equally proud of his design.

### #14. "Laminated Leaves"

*Procedure:*

Here is a suggestion for your use. The leftover leaves and plants from all your art projects can be laminated or covered with plastic. Preferably, the machine should not be used, but there are several plastics at school supply houses that stick together in the same way.

Once they are covered, cut them out about one-fourth to

one-half inch away from the leaves. Save these for bulletin board use. They specifically can be used for a calendar. By using an erasable ink, you can write the number of each day of the month on them. You may also write names of helpers and leaders on them. They can be used as fillers on the bulletin board and, if cut out carefully, they can be used for stencils around which the children can trace.

### #15. "Tree of the Month"

*Procedure:*

Find a limb of a tree or a small bush that has several small branches on it. If you live where manzanita grows, you have a perfect specimen. Take the bark off and it is all ready. If you use a different plant, spray it with shellac to keep it from breaking up sooner than it normally would.

Using a container that will hold up your plant, pour plaster of Paris around the plant, filling up the container. When the plaster is dry you have a plant that can be decorated in many different ways. The best method to use in kindergarten is to hang small objects on the limbs as if from a mobile.

The objects must be no more than three or four inches in length, and should be made by the children. A hole punched through the object, then a short string through the hole and tied to a limb, completes the process. You will not be able to use every child's work every month, but groups can take turns. Some ideas for the months are:

| | |
|---|---|
| September: | leaves |
| October: | ghosts, owls, bats, witches, pumpkins |
| November: | turkeys or Indians made from hand patterns |
| December: | any tree decorations |
| January: | snowflakes, mittens, caps |
| February: | valentines |
| March: | kites |

April:              umbrellas

May:                flowers

June:               birds, bees, flowers

July:               flags

August:             sun, beach umbrellas, bathing suits

July and August are included for teachers who teach in year-round school systems.

#16. "Rock Objects"

*Procedure:*

If you will go to a stream, river, or ocean shore where small rocks can be found, pick up lots of small ones, three or four inches in width, and the same amount of rocks about half that size. Round or oval shapes are best. The purpose for going to the water is that rocks in water have often been worn smooth.

Give each child two rocks—one of the larger and one of the smaller. Ask the children to look at them, place the small one on the larger, and try to visualize an animal, fowl, or other object. When they decide on their subject, they will paint the rocks accordingly. When dry, the children glue (you must have a good glue) the little one onto the larger. Allow this to dry thoroughly. The following day, the children may add facial features and other characteristics of their subject, such as wings, tails, facial features, etc. They should use felt markers that have thin tips. Spray the object with shellac. These make lovely gifts for anyone and for any occasion.

## Creating with Ordinary School Supplies

There are so many things one can have kindergarteners create from paint that it would be impossible to name them all. Try the following activities often, varying the exercises in different ways. Add your new ideas to your file cards along with the different occasions with which the projects are particularly suitable

#### #17. "Blotto Prints"

*Objectives:*

1. To create lovely objects with little expense.
2. To develop coordination.
3. To improve visual perception and interpretative skills.
4. To improve language skills.

*Procedure:*

Almost everyone has done some form of print blots. These are made by folding a piece of paper in half and painting on just one side. Folding the other side over and spreading all the paint outward from one point finishes the project. When opened, the results never cease to amaze youngsters.

Names written on one side can be reversed on the other. Objects can also be reprinted. When studying transportation, always draw one half of a vehicle on one side. If the top is drawn at the center, the vehicle can be cut out around the wheels and sides. Fold it in the center again, but this time fold with the paint side up. Now the children have an automobile that will stand up and is painted on both sides.

To make absolutely beautiful butterfly shapes, give each child a large sheet of butcher paper. Now let each child pour a small amount of paint in the center fold. If the children are given small amounts of two colors that form other colors, such as yellow and red, the resulting form will have three colors. This is very striking and lovely. Be sure that the children smooth out all the paint, rubbing in all directions.

The following day, give each child a felt marker that contrasts with the colors in his shape. Let each youngster trace around his figure and cut it out. If the edges are too jagged, you, or your helpers, will need to cut them out for the children, especially for the uncoordinated ones.

### #18. "Dip It"

*Procedure:*

Make up two or three colors of thin tempera paint of bright colors. Put the paint in small containers, about one to one-and-a-half inches deep. Give each child a white napkin (you probably have some in the room) or a sheet torn from a roll of paper towels. Fold this in half twice. The children now dip the corners into different colors of paint. When the multi-colored napkins are opened and allowed to dry, they can be used for various things, such as borders for bulletin boards, as a backing for smaller items on bulletin boards, or as a lining for baskets, particularly Easter and flower baskets. The tie-dye effect makes these lovely, and every child's will be beautiful.

### #19. "Color and Wash"

*Procedure:*

For special days, let the children draw a picture on a colored sheet of construction paper with the same color of crayon. For instance, on Valentine's Day each child can draw a special valentine for another child in the room, using a white crayon on white construction paper. The crayon is hard to see. The drawing is now exchanged with a friend, who paints over it with red water color or thin tempera. The entire sheet is covered with the paint, and all in the same color. When dry, (the thin paint will not take long) each child may cut out his valentine to take home with him.

In the winter, let the children draw snow scenes with a black crayon on black paper. When exchanged, the children paint over them with white paint. Any number of objects can be made with white on white and then painted over with the appropriate color.

Remind the children often that they will need to press down with their crayon in order for their secret to show.

#20. "Blow Painting"

*Procedure:*

Place a tiny amount of tempera paint at the bottom of a sheet of construction paper. If the children dip their straws in paint and let it drop on their paper in the appropriate spot, there will be sufficient paint for blowing. They now use the straw, blowing through it, to push the paint up and out in all directions to form tree shapes. The color of the paint will depend upon the object for which it is to be used: brown for trees, green for bushes or flowers, any color for underwater coral, etc. When these are dry, they can be finished into complete scenes in different ways. For instance, if it is an underwater scene, blue water color can be painted over the entire scene. If the design includes trees, flowers, or other plants, the children may dab on paint with brushes in places where leaves and the flowers are located. Finger prints are lovely when made into leaves and flowers. Or, use the following suggestion to finish the scene.

#21. "Sponge Painting"

*Procedure:*

Most teachers have used sponge painting at one time or another. It is an easy and quick way to finish a scene. Anytime you have old sponges that begin to break apart, tear some into small pieces and leave others in larger pieces. Store in a container to use for sponge prints. The sponge pieces are dipped into paint and dabbed lightly on the paper to make the desired design.

The preceding activity is a perfect one to finish with sponge painting. For trees in fall, all the autumn colors may be used. Green will be used in spring along with pink blossoms. Designing on wrapping paper can also be done. Repeat patterns are excellent for developing visual discrimination. For this, make a pattern on a large sheet of paper. The children should study it and duplicate it. Start with simple patterns, then proceed to more complicated ones when the children are ready for them. Any drawing with crayons can be set off by adding a few dabs of sponge painting.

## #22. "Dragged Abstracts"

*Procedure:*

On a smooth surface, counter top, linoleum, or oilcloth, put small dabs of three colors of paint. About a half-teaspoon is enough of each color. Experiment with colors until you get the combination you desire. Let each child wet a sheet of butcher paper or fingerpaint paper. This is easily done if you put an inch or so of water in a sink. The paint should be nearby. The children should hold up the paper over the sink, let it drip, then lay it on top of the paint. The paper is then wiggled and twisted back and forth until most of the paper is covered. Finally, lay the prints on newspapers to dry.

These prints will now be used to make greeting cards. Out of tagboard, cut the shape you desire to put on the card. Cut out the center of this shape, leaving a frame of at least one-half inch. This frame now becomes a "finder." With student and parent helpers, let each child move the finder around on his print to find the spot he wants for his card. With help to hold the frame in place, he now traces around the inside of the frame. This one part is now cut from the drag print, and the rest are discarded unless you wish to make more than one card with them.

The part cut out is now glued to a card of white construction paper that has been folded into fourths. In order to put a frame around the outside of the print, ditto a frame that is just a fraction smaller on the inside than the original frame. Put this on a contrasting color. When the children carefully cut it out, it should be glued around the print on the card; being a bit smaller on the inside, this outer frame will cover the edges of the print.

If these prints are made in late spring, the children should be able to write a message inside. For example, they can write "Be my Valentine," "Happy Mother's Day," or "Happy Easter," depending on the occasion. The children now sign their name and take their lovely card home.

These always look pretty regardless of who makes them. They make lovely cards for you to make to send to people. Just add a message inside, and you will not find a prettier card anywhere. They sound as if they are a lot of work, but they actually are not. Any shape can be used for the frame finder. It will depend on the occasion. For Valentine's Day, a heart shape can be used. At Christmas, a tree or bell shape is appropriate. A rectangular shape that covers most of the card is very pretty. Cover the rest of the card with a black frame, and it looks very professional.

## #23. "Tissue Dab"

*Procedure:*

Let each child wet a piece of butcher or fingerpaint paper as in the previous activity. They should then brush tempera paint over it quickly with a wide brush. If you put two colors of tempera together without stirring thoroughly, the effects will be prettier.

After the paint has been put on, the children should use a facial tissue and dab over the paper, taking up the paint here and there. This provides a stippling effect, leaving light and shadow areas. Short and curved strokes, quick dabs, or special designs can be used. The results are always lovely. Do not let the children work at this so long that they start tearing the paper.

When these are dry, they may be used for bulletin board displays on a contrasting background, or, as the background for other bulletin board items. The frame finder used in the last activity could also be employed here. The parts cut out can be used for greeting cards.

## Using Odds and Ends to the Delight of Kindergarteners

It is probably said of kindergarten teachers that we are scavengers. And it is true! Not one of us would think of letting something go to waste just because there was only a dab left. A dab here and a dab there can make lovely art projects.

*Objectives for procedures 24-29:*

1. To enjoy a creation and to promote creativity.
2. To develop coordination.
3. To increase visual perception.
4. To improve language skills.

## #24. "Cloth Printing"

*Procedure:*

To print on cloth, all one needs is cloth and felt markers with unwashable ink. If the cloth is not going to be washed, the water-soluble ink may be used. Let the children practice on scraps before they attempt a special project. If nothing else, they can trace around objects on a printed piece of fabric.

To make articles, the children must exercise care in order to achieve a pleasing finished article. This is why practice is a must. Provide stencils (templates) for the children to trace around when they make their article.

For example, if the class is making Christmas stockings, stencils with the appropriate-sized Christmas ornaments should be provided. Each child helps another by holding the template in place as the other traces around it carefully. It is best to have some embroidery hoops to hold the fabric taut when the printing is done. Perhaps enough mothers have them that you will have enough for several to be working at a time.

Valentines made of red felt or other heavy material can be decorated with smaller hearts by tracing small templates in a pleasing pattern over the larger heart. These may then be glued to a card to take home.

## #25. "Stringing Straws"

*Procedure:*

Buy several blunt-point needles. They are large, easily

threaded, and not dangerous when children are taught how to use them carefully. Next, you will need to cut up several striped drinking straws into about one-inch pieces. Older students can do this for you, or the children can do it themselves.

Depending on the use you are going to make of these, you will need to provide the children with something that will go between each piece of straw as the children string them with yarn or heavy thread. If they are going to be used for kite tails or bulletin board borders, a simple inch square of colored construction paper between each straw is very pretty. Or, if you have lots of odd buttons that have been donated to the class, they will go beautifully with the straws.

Small hearts cut out by the children (most learn to do this free hand) and put between the straw pieces make excellent decorations in February. Small shamrocks and straws in March can be used for decorations and kite tails. A flower shape for May, pumpkins for November, or bells for Christmas are just a few of the possibilities.

This activity provides the children with a lot of cutting and stringing practice, which is especially beneficial for coordination development and visual perceptiveness.

### #26. "Straw Pictures"

*Procedures:*

Using paper straws with the same striped pattern as used in the previous activity, let the children cut their own pieces to the size they need to glue onto paper to make trees, flowers, buildings, fences, etc. (See Figure 7-4.) A flower stem would be longer than the leaves. Tree trunks with branches of shorter straws or bushes with limbs of straws that branch out from the bottom are just two examples of what can be done. Blossoms and leaves may be cut out of construction paper and added to the scene; sponge-painted leaves and flowers are another possibility; but the prettiest would be tissue leaves and blossoms.

Using round pieces of tissue paper about one inch in width, show the children how to put the circle around their finger, dip it in the glue very lightly, and glue this where the leaves and blossoms should be. The tissue paper and the striped straws make lovely bulletin board displays when used to make up a scene. The tissue paper stands up even higher than the straws, giving the creation a three-dimensional effect.

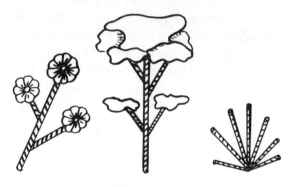

**Figure 7-4**

## #27. "Paper-Clip Necklaces"

*Procedure:*

As a gift for Mother's Day, why not let the children make paper-clip necklaces? Give the children several paper clips and show them how to put them together. It will take some children longer to learn than others, but all can do it. It is a very good coordination development exercise.

Each child puts enough clips together to make a necklace of average length. (It should slip over the head easily.) With help from older students, they now cover each clip with the colored tape one can buy in stores. You can buy a width that is just right to cover the clips with only the points showing. The children will need help in determining the proper length of tape to wrap around the clips; just enough to cover and overlap a bit is sufficient.

Adhesive-backed paper in mottled colors can also make very pretty necklaces—even prettier than the tape. However, you need to use a fresh roll from which to cut the strips to cover the clips. Rolls that have been open a while do not always remain stuck to the clips. You can test a few clips and leave them . overnight to see if your paper sticks well.

#28. "Paper Cup Art"

*Procedure:*

Paper cups used for baking are even more versatile as an art form. The illustrations show some of the many forms that any child will be able to make. (See Figure 7-5.)

**Figure 7-5**

The umbrella starts out with the children providing a handle made of construction paper, pipe cleaners, or paper straw. The three cups are folded in half twice and stapled to the construction paper on which they are being placed. They should be stapled under the top layer; this holds all the layers down yet allows the top layer to blouse out. Drops of rain cut out of light blue construction paper can be added to finish the picture.

To make a flower that is blooming, the children first provide a stem and leaves, which can be made of construction paper, rickrack, yarn, or any other choice you may have. The bottom flower, being the first to bloom, is in full bloom. Therefore, the paper cup is glued as is—sitting flat. The second flower is half open, so we fold the paper cup in half and glue or staple the bottom part to the paper. The others are still in the bud stage, so we fold them in fourths or even tighter. These may need to be stapled; use your judgment.

Animals and human forms can be constructed with similar ease. Try those here and make up others.

#### #29. "Cookie Art"

*Procedure:*

On holidays when you are having treats and parties, let the children decorate cookies or cupcakes. This makes the treat an extra special one as they have helped prepare it.

For example, suppose you have mothers who want to bake cookies for Halloween. Tell the mothers to make plain cookies, make up orange icing, and bring raisins, chocolate drops, or candy corns for the children to make the facial features on a jack-o'-lantern cookie. The icing should be of a consistency that will spread easily but should not be runny. With mothers to help the children, the children may use plastic knives to spread the icing on the cookies. The facial features can then be added.

Maybe you will have cupcakes for a Valentine's Day treat. Tell the mothers to bring white icing and little red heart candies for trimming the cupcake.

At the kindergarten level, children enjoy doing something similar to this activity for their parties rather than to play games. They are much too excited to settle down to playing games. Creating something to eat is a different thing! And the children are learning. They develop visual and interpretative skills while improving their coordination. Try it. You will like it too!

Other art activities are throughout the book. Since art must be a personal endeavor, you should interpret the activities in this chapter according to your needs and to your children's needs. Make a file of ideas and, when you try one, jot down any special tips you have found to make them more beneficial. Above all, enjoy art with your students!

# 8

## Using Games and Related Activities to Develop Kindergarten Skills

### Key Roles Games Play in the Kindergarten Program

Games and related activities are fundamental to a well-rounded kindergarten curriculum. The elements of excitement, movement, and participation are the chief factors. It is the rare youngster who does not readily enter into games.

The advancement of large and small motor skills, plus the improvement of social and emotional attitudes developed through cooperative adventures, makes games in kindergarten a must.

You have used some of these games before. Nevertheless, try them again using the suggested changes.

### Games and Activities Adaptable to Classroom and Party Use

*Objectives:*

These are the objectives for most of the games in this chapter. Some will not apply to every activity.

147

1. To develop coordination.
2. To improve language skills.
3. To develop cooperation and other social skills.
4. To offer activities that develop fundamental skills in experiences that are not threatening.
5. To add fun and excitement to the curriculum.
6. To develop concentration.
7. To develop visual perception.
8. To develop auditory perception.

### #1. "Pass It"

*Procedure:*

It is suggested that small groups participate in this game, with helpers to direct the procedures. It can, however, be played with the entire group.

This game is like the game of "Gossip," except no words are spoken. Each child tries to get the next child to laugh, smile, or giggle. If any child does, he is out. The one staying in the game the longest is the winner and may start the next game.

The first child does something to the next, who repeats the same procedure to the next child, and so on. The action done must be simple and for the purpose of making the other child laugh. It should be something like a tickle on the chin, a funny facial expression, etc. Require that the children do something that takes only a few seconds to complete in order to keep the game moving quickly.

### #2. "Holiday Charades"

*Procedure:*

During holiday months after the children have learned to do charades, let groups of two or three children get together and decide on something pertaining to the holiday that they would like to imitate, such as objects, animals, or people. After a few minutes practice time, have all the children come together. One by one, each group will act out their part. For instance, if the holiday is Thanksgiving, one group may be turkeys, another may be the Indians coming to the feast, another may be the Pilgrims, and others may portray the eating, the games, or the cooking and clean-up. The other children must try to guess what each group is pretending to be or do.

This activity is a good way to review a unit on holidays, as the children must remember the details in order to carry out the assignment. It can also be used for other units unrelated to holidays.

### #3. "Monkey See, Monkey Do"

*Procedure:*

This activity is similar to charades. Have small groups of children decide on some action to perform for the others. A simple activity such as washing windows, sweeping the floor, peeling potatoes, diapering a baby, driving a car, cutting wood, etc., is the type needed for this game. Stories or nursery rhymes are too long.

As the group starts the pantomime, the audience (the other children) begin to mimic them, trying to guess what the activity is. As soon as someone guesses, another group performs.

### #4. "Finish It"

*Procedure:*

This activity is often done by older students, but there is no reason why kindergarten children should not do it too.

Start a picture on the board. It may be part of a tree in your mind, but since you only draw a short line, the first child may think it is part of a face. He may add another line which he thinks is a chin, the next child may add something, and so on, until some object appears. The last children will add finishing touches. When everyone has a turn, it is fun to tell what each thought the subject was going to be before the final object appeared.

Keep the children moving. If some children cannot think of something to add and cannot add it quickly, let others draw until the slower ones get an idea. This game is very good for small groups of children, especially those who have difficulty thinking quickly and those who think less creatively. If it is done often enough, they will improve in their creative ability.

### #5. "The Groundhog and the Dogs"

*Procedure:*

Explain the theory behind Groundhog Day to the children. Next, select one child to be the groundhog; all the others will be the dogs. The groundhog finds a "hole" somewhere in the classroom. This can be beside a chair, behind the desk, anywhere, as long as all the children know that the groundhog is home and is safe from the "dogs."

The dogs are seated ten or more feet away from the hole. When the groundhog comes out, the children must all stay seated until the teacher yells, "Dogs!" Now all the children try to catch the groundhog before he gets back to his hole. If someone catches him, he may be the next groundhog. The trick to this is that everyone is down on all fours; they must all move as the animals do.

### #6. "Blind Draw"

*Procedure:*

If you do not have blindfolds for each child, it is suggested you get some or make them. My previous book has included a way for making blindfolds, and the children find them exciting to wear. They are useful for many activities, especially games.

Give each child a piece of paper and a crayon. The children put on their masks and draw a simple object. The subject of the picture will depend upon the purpose. For instance, if this is a party for Halloween, let the children draw pumpkins; for Valentine's Day, let them draw a heart; for Easter, they can draw an egg; for March, a kite; for Christmas, a tree; and so on.

If prizes are being given to everyone for some event during a party, you may want to give a prize for the most realistic drawing, for the funniest, the biggest, and so on.

Give the children several tries at drawing the object, and give prizes to different children each time.

#### #7. "Find the Change"

*Procedure:*

Have all the children form a circle. One child stands in the center and looks at every child, trying to fix in his mind where everyone is standing. He then puts on a blindfold and turns around two or three times. Two children quietly exchange places. When someone says, "Ready," the child in the center uncovers his eyes and tries to discover the change. If he cannot guess, he is told. Another child now takes his place. It would be best to do this in small groups before including all the children in one large group.

If you divide the class into small groups, the same procedure may be used with letters, numbers, shapes, colors, or anything that can be written or glued onto a large card. For instance, give each child a card on which you have written a different numeral. When the blindfold is placed on the child, two other children exchange cards. When the blindfold is removed, the child tries to find the two differently placed cards. If your groups are small enough, the children will soon become adept at seeing these changes. As they improve in memory, increase the size of the group.

#### #8. "Mary's Lost Lamb"

*Procedure:*

"Oh, dear. Mary has lost her lamb!" Not really, but that is the name of the game.

Mary, or Harry, says, "I lost my lamb. Will you help me find it?" The other children ask, "What did it look like?" The child then describes one of the children in the room while the others try to guess who the "lamb" is.

An older student sitting away from the others can help the children with their descriptions if they need it. While Mary is talking to the children, another child is being advised about the description that he wishes to give. The children should be encouraged to give their own descriptions, but they also must know enough about another child to describe him without looking at him. Therefore, with the aid of your helper, the activity can move quickly, allowing more children the opportunity to participate.

As the children learn to describe someone in detail, beginning with the facial features and progressing to clothing, they should soon be able to play this game without the aid of anyone.

This game may prove valuable to the children if they are ever called upon to give a description of someone. Though we do not like to think of such things happening to children, crimes are often committed to or around them, and their descriptions of a suspect may be very important. This game can be played in connection with warnings about staying away from strangers and the importance of their descriptions if someone should try to bother them in any way.

### #9. "Tom Thumb's Hide-Out"

*Procedure:*

One child—Tom Thumb—tells the teacher where he is hiding. Since Tom is so small, he may be hiding anywhere—behind a doorknob, in a light fixture, in a pencil sharpener, etc. The other children try to guess where he is.

Tom and the teacher should tell the children the general area, or the game could go on forever. The children may also ask questions concerning that area.

## Favorite Games That Develop Coordination

### #10. "Hot Potato"

*Procedure:*

Everyone knows how to play this game, which requires the children to quickly pass a ball around a circle. The child holding the ball when the whistle blows is out, or you may play a selection of music and stop it occasionally.

In order to develop both large and small motor control, let us change the game somewhat. Of course, start with large balls, but later add anything that requires special handling such as hula hoops, jump ropes, large blocks, boxes, etc. Space the children in a circle commensurate with the object used. For example, using a hula hoop, the children should be spaced at least two arm's lengths apart.

The children will find that handling these special items requires certain considerations. For instance, they will quickly learn that if they do not fold the jump rope it will always be dragging on the floor. Once an article touches the floor, the child responsible is out.

After using the larger articles, try smaller ones. Small balls, bean bags, marbles, buttons, beans, small rocks etc., may all be used. The children will need to be closer together in the circle when using the smaller items.

### #11. "Find a Base"

*Procedure:*

The children form a large circle. About two feet inside the circle, an article is placed in front of each child. One child stands in the middle, but no object is placed in the circle for him. The articles may be bean bags, hula hoops or rubber number and alphabet stepping stones. The stepping stones are best, as they do not slide.

Play a recording of a rhythmic activity. The children should move around the circle accordingly. For instance, if the recording is a skipping rhythm, the children skip; if it is a galloping rhythm, the children gallop, and so on. When the music stops, everyone tries to put a foot on one of the articles in the circle. The child in the center must find one too. The child left without an object is the next one in the center.

Or, the game can be played as musical chairs. Make the large circle, but with no one in the center. Place the articles inside. Start by placing one less than the number of children, and each time the music stops, remove another article. Each time one child will be out. The child staying in the longest is the winner. To avoid the depressing feeling of being left out, allow a "loser" to sit in the center of the circle to help "judge." Do this for any game that requires children to leave, such as in the game of "Hot Potato."

### #12. "Leap Frog"

*Procedure:*

When you first teach children to play Leap Frog, have the children form a large circle with at least two arm's lengths between each child. Next, have the children face in one direction and assume the frog position. Show them how to get in a position that best protects their heads. As the first child goes over the second child, the second gets up and follows, and so on around. As the children complete the circle, they again get down into the frog position for others to jump over them. It would be best not to play this game too long at first, as it is a tiring game.

This game is particularly useful for teaching the term *over* in math. When you have other positional terms to teach in math, add obstacle courses for the children in order to teach additional terms. For instance, if you are teaching the meaning of the word *under*, set up an easel in such a way that each child must go under it before leaping over the next child. Naturally, you will not set up an obstacle between every child. A few here and there will be sufficient.

If you are teaching the term *into* or *inside of,* lay some old tires around the circle for the children to step into before going over the next child. If the term is *around,* set up blocks or small chairs for the children to go around before proceeding to the next child.

Obstacle courses are particularly intriguing to children anyway. Different types of obstacle courses that teach various math terms make good activities without playing Leap Frog. The following activity is just one of the many ways this can be done.

### #13. "Follow the Leader"

*Procedure:*

Record rhythm music on a tape. Change rhythms about every two minutes. For instance, you may start with skipping; the next rhythm may be galloping; then hopping, and so on. As you are recording, add instructions for the children to follow when they play this game.

In this activity you are concerned with the reinforcement of math terms. Therefore, as you are recording, you should occasionally give such instructions on the tape as "Go around the largest block," "Go under the table," "Go between the two chairs," "Step inside the hula hoop," "Go through the hula hoop" (this can be done by taping a hoop upright bwtween two chairs to keep it from falling), "Go beside the tallest chair," "Go over the shortest block," and so on. The children are to continue the rhythm pattern as they carry out the instructions. For instance, if they are hopping, they will continue to hop as they go through the loop.

The drawback to this activity is that you will have to set up various obstacles around the room before you record, in order to know what you are going to use and how they will be used to stress specific math terms. However, this is not a big problem as there are tables, chairs, blocks, easels, etc., that are readily available in your classroom. It will simply be a matter of putting them around the room. It will not matter if the children do have to go all the way across the room to carry out an instruction. Space out your instructions so one does not follow another so closely that the leader does not have enough time to execute the preceding activity. Change leaders occasionally so several children can share the responsibility of leading others.

#### #14. "Dodge Ball"

*Procedure:*

Dodge ball can be fun, but the children can also get hurt unless they are careful in throwing the ball. Use a large sponge ball to avoid injuries. Dodge ball is excellent for building coordination and for recognizing oneself in relation to space.

If you have a helper, divide the children into two groups. Find a marked area for each group of children. If there is no marked area, draw a large circle for each group, one at a good distance from the other. As each group goes to the dodge-ball area, divide the smaller groups into halves—half of the children on one team, half on the other; half will get inside the circle, half will stand outside to throw the ball as they try to hit someone inside. As each child is hit, he must leave the circle and join the group on the outside of the circle. When all children have been hit, the teams exchange places and repeat the process.

To change this game, have all the children within the circle sit down. The circle will need to be very large, and it should be on a relatively clean surface. The team on the outside of the circle must roll the ball across the floor as they try to hit the children inside. The children inside should be continually watching in order to get up and move out of the way of the ball. Any other positional change for the team inside the circle may be made. Also, changes in the manner of moving the ball through the circle may be made.

### Developing Skills Through Races

#### #15. "Simple Races"

*Procedure:*

Using any activity requiring movement, let children race to a specified location. Be sure they are as evenly matched as possible. A well-coordinated child should be placed with others of the same caliber. Likewise, children who are uncoordinated should be matched with similar children.

It is best to have older students take small groups of equally matched children to a specific area to carry out races. By so doing, all the children can be participating most of the time rather than waiting their turn. Most discipline problems arise during inactivity rather than during an activity, regardless of what the activity is.

Some simple races may include:

1. Running, jumping, hopping, skipping, galloping, etc.
2. Jumping rope at a run; walking with a hula hoop moving around the waist.
3. Bouncing balls while moving.
4. Kicking balls from one line to another. To make this more difficult, require that the ball stop on the line. If it goes over, the children must kick it back to the line.
5. Carrying bean bags on the head, hands, and shoulders.
6. Any others you wish to add.

## #16. "Complex Races"

*Procedure:*

Complex races include those that require more than one child to accomplish and those that are more difficult for the children. These types of races must be done after simple ones have been mastered.

1. The Wheelbarrow race involves two children—one holds the legs of the other, who walks on his hands from one place to another. For kindergarten children the distance should be short. It is important that children are matched with someone of equal size.
2. The Crabwalk involves only one child, but he must walk with his hands and feet on the floor behind him, stomach and face turned upward.

Carryall races involve the carrying of some article in a specified manner. For instance:

3. The children may race a short distance with a ball between the knees.

4. Give each participant two or three balls, depending on size, and have him carry them with his arms around the balls. His hands should not touch. If a ball is dropped, the child must stop and put it back with the others before continuing.

5. A stack of three or four blocks must be carried from one point to another. The stack must be balanced on the hands, not held against the person.

6. Any other similar activity that will aid in the development of both large and small coordination.

#### #17. "Group Races"

*Procedure:*

Any race can involve groups of students. It would be better, however, if a class of thirty kindergarteners could be divided into at least four groups. Two groups can participate under the direction of an aide or parent. Two other groups can be under your direction. Some interesting group races may be:

1. Carrying beanbags on the head, shoulders, backs or hands, on the feet, etc., without the aid of hands. If one child drops his, the others may go ahead, but they cannot win the race until all participants reach the goal line. The first group having all members at the goal line first is the winner.

2. Dribbling balls. The children must dribble the balls all the way. If a child loses his ball, he must get it and return to the approximate place where he lost the ball before he can continue.

3. Pitching balls. This activity requires partners within the group. Each pair of partners may be spaced close together, but they must pitch the ball from one to another

as they move from one line to another. A group cannot win unless all sets of partners are at the finish line. This is also good to use with only two sets of partners.

4. Twirling hula hoops. All children have a hula hoop twirling about the waist, and they must be doing some other activity with their feet such as running or skipping.

5. Jumping ropes while running. This is not too difficult for children who jump rope, but if a child does not jump well, he may have difficulty. Again, all the children must be at the finish line to win.

6. Add other group races that you like.

## Relays That Add Excitement to Learning

In relays, half the students are lined up to compete against the other half. Each child must accomplish the same task and each group must strive to complete the activity before the other.

A starting line, clearly marked with tape or some other substance, is very important. If a goal line is required, it also must be clearly marked.

In kindergarten classes, it is advisable to divide the children into two groups, one group with the teacher and the other with an aide. These groups are then subdivided in order to have two equal groups of team members. Although it is not necessary to divide your class for all relays, some of these activities take a long time to complete, and those children not participating may become restless. Therefore, it is suggested that relays be done when you have an aide, parent, or student who can help you.

#### #18. "Jack's Candlestick"

*Procedure:*

Each group of children is lined up behind a starting line. In front of each group, about six feet from the starting line, place an object that represents the candle.

Each child is numbered according to his position in the line. Each must run and jump over the candle calling out his number as he does. If he fails to say his number, he must go back to the starting line and repeat the process.

Each child must wait until the one in front of him is over the candle before he starts running. If he starts before, he will have to go back.

As the children go over the candle, have them stand to the side of their team until all have completed the relay. The winning team is the one whose members all complete the process first.

As a variation, have each child jump as many times as the numeral he says represents.

### #19. "Sweep"

*Procedure:*

Divide the children into two groups. Line each group up behind a starting line. About eight feet from the line, place a cardboard box upside down in front of each group—two boxes are necessary. In the side facing the children, a hole should be cut at the bottom of the box. (See Figure 8-1.)

Give a broom to the first child in each row. Put some object on the starting line. The objective requires each child to sweep the article to the box and into the hole. He then runs with the broom and gives it to the next person in line. A duplicate object is waiting for this child. A helper may get the objects from the boxes, but you should have at least two available for each team. This will prevent delays.

The object to be swept may be anything that will move easily over the surface on which the game is played. Blocks, small balls, marbles, buttons, small rocks, etc., are only a few examples.

This game requires the children to think before they act. The object can easily go beyond the box, in which case the child must sweep it back to the front of the box and into the hole. Hands may not be used to move the object from one place to another unless it lodges under something. The first team whose members complete the process is the winner.

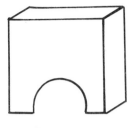

**Figure 8-1**

#20. "Pass This and That"

*Procedure:*

Place two rows of tape about six feet or more apart. Each group will line up behind the tape, facing each other. Place several small items such as one-inch balls, buttons, blocks, etc., in a box or other container at one end of each row, the same items in each box. At the other end of each row, place an empty container.

On a signal to start, the first child picks up one object and passes it to the next child. It passes consecutively from one child to another, and it must be placed in every child's hand. The last child drops the article into the empty container.

As soon as the first child passes an object to the next child, he quickly gets another object and passes it along. He must act quickly, but he cannot have more than one object in his hand at any time.

When all the articles are in the second box, the first child on that end starts them back up the line, one by one. When all objects are back in their original starting place, the task is completed. The winner is the first team to have all the objects back in the original container.

#21. "Touch Relay"

*Procedure:*

The two groups are lined up behind a starting line. The first child in each row runs to a pre-determined goal line, then runs back and touches the hand of the second child, who repeats the process, and so on, until all children have completed the activity.

Change this simple relay to any other form of physical activity that you wish. Besides running, you may want the children to skip, hop on one foot, hop on both feet, leap, slide, crawl, gallop, hop as a rabbit, walk as an elephant, leap as a kangaroo, etc. This change allows you to evaluate each child's progress in several different areas. If you are evaluating the children, the aide should mark one check list for her group while you mark the one for your group.

### #22. "Pass Relay"

*Procedure:*

The two groups are lined up in two rows, one child behind another. The object of this game is to pass some object from one child to another in a pre-determined manner. On receiving the article, the last child in the row runs to the front of the line and the process is repeated. This continues until the first child is back in his original place. The first group to complete this procedure is the winner.

Any article that can be passed is suitable to use in this game. Large balls should be used first. Add smaller articles that will require the use of the smaller muscles to manipulate them, such as small balls, bean bags, blocks, marbles, buttons, etc.

Vary the procedure for passing the objects. Some ideas are:

1. Passing over the head of each person.
2. Passing between the legs of each child.
3. Alternately passing over the head and between the legs.
4. Passing over the head while in a sitting position.
5. Alternately passing to the side of one child and crossing over and psssing down the opposite side of the next child while in a sitting or standing position.
6. Passing from hands to hands while lying on the back.

When receiving the object, the last child must get up, run to the head of the line, and lie down before passing it to the next child.

7. Alternately passing the object in front of one child and behind the next while each group is facing each other in a sitting position. Do the same while standing, facing each other.

8. Make up other combinations.

Games can be one of the most beneficial avenues open to you. They are effective reinforcement exercises, they require very little equipment, they can be adapted to your special needs, and they are fun and exhilarating. Use them as often as you can. Time spent in game participation is not wasted. Change them! Use them! Enjoy them!

# 9

## Laying the Foundation for Scientific Exploration in Kindergarten

### Why Science Is Important in the Kindergarten Curriculum

One of the main purposes of science activities in kindergarten is to guide the children to an awareness of their environment. Another objective is to begin the development of a language background that will aid the children in the understanding of the processes involved in the changes that take place in nature.

If, as kindergarten teachers, we are able to foster an inquisitiveness about the marvelous happenings in nature, we will have laid a foundation for future scientific exploration.

Although many other scientific experiences could have been included in this chapter, most of the activities center around the different seasons. The same types of activities should be engaged in to emphasize the other realms of science.

## Techniques That Contribute to Scientific Language Skills While Learning About Autumn

Because of the popularity of activities featured in musical recordings, this chapter again refers you outside this book for the recommended supplies. As explained in Chapter 6, these exhilarating recordings make learning about any subject, and in this case science, an active and exciting process. Those mentioned in this chapter are equally as popular with the children.

### #1. "The Search"

*Objectives:*

1. To develop awareness of the surroundings.
2. To increase vocabulary.
3. To develop perceptual skills.
4. To enjoy a learning situation.

*Procedure:*

Tell the children that they are going for a walk to search for words. This will stimulate enough curiosity to be able to explain what the children are expected to do and why. Take the children to a specified area to look at the surroundings, to touch and to smell things. They must be very observant of their environment in order to provide special words for how things look, smell, sound, and feel. The beginning of the spring and fall units is a particularly good time to take walks to grassy areas where trees, shrubs, and wild flowers are growing.

After the children arrive at the place, allow them to explore for several minutes. Bring them together and have them sit down and give you words that describe how they perceive their surroundings. You should write these words down to be used in follow-up exercises.

**#2. "Autumn Leaves" and "Autumn is Here"**
(by Lucille Wood and Louise Scott from *More Singing Fun*, Volume I, Bowman Records, Inc.)

*Objectives for procedures 2-3:*

1. To review the actions observed on the walk in the previous example.
2. To participate in the action of fall activities.
3. To enjoy a lesson that emphasizes fall characteristics.
4. To develop coordination.

*Procedure:*

If the walk you took in the first example was taken in the fall, allow the children to participate in these two recordings on returning to the classroom. The actions performed will remind them of things they learned on their trip. After the exercise, ask the children if they can think of any more words that would relate to the fall season. If so, write them down with the others.

**#3. "Pretty Roses" and "Fuzzy Wuzzy Caterpillar"**
(by Douglas and Gloria Evans from *Physical Fitness*, Kimbo Records.)

*Procedure:*

If the walk is in the late spring, these two recordings are excellent to reinforce the concepts the children were introduced to on their trip. If possible, while on the trip, show the children roses that are beginning to grow and caterpillars on plants. Ask the children how they think a caterpillar feels as he goes through all the processes to become a butterfly. (Be sure you have explained all the cycles before asking.)

Following the music lesson, let the children engage in the following art project if it is autumn. If it is spring, make up similar word pictures.

#4. "Word Pictures"

*Objectives:*

1. To reinforce word meanings.
2. To involve critical thinking skills.
3. To enjoy an art project while learning science terms.
4. To develop coordination.

*Procedure:*

While you are on such word hunts, let the children collect leaves, stems, nuts, nut shells, flowers, etc., that they might find on the ground to use in art projects.

When the children return to the classroom, and the things collected have been divided among the different tables, give each table of children a different word picture to draw. They may use the collage materials collected in the pictures as all or part of the scene. Some suggestions for autumn word pictures, using the words the children related to you on the trip, are to produce a picture of:

1. A tree with red, yellow, and orange leaves swirling and twirling about it as if they were dancing to music.
2. A dandelion with its white whiskers, while a child who pretends to be the wind sends its soft, feathery seeds flying through the air.
3. How the ground looks as a strong wind comes rushing through the bright-colored leaves, giving them a ride on its wings which no one can see.
4. The bushes as they wave to all the world as the wind moves their whispering branches back and forth.

Follow the same procedure for the other seasons.

## #5. "Bouquets"

*Objectives for procedures 5-6:*

1. To reinforce science language skills.
2. To engage in art projects.
3. To promote understanding.

*Procedure:*

When pretty, colored leaves are found, tell the children to leave the stems on in order to use them in this project. Let the children lay the prettiest leaves between pages of old newspapers. When these have dried, spray them with shellac or other liquid plastic.

Late in the fall, or even into the other seasons, these leaves make beautiful additions to bouquets. They can also be made into bouquets as gifts for others. What a joy it would be for older people in rest homes if the kindergarteners made them a bouquet of brightly colored leaves with possibly one plastic flower among them. By taking these to the homes themselves, the children would learn a lot about real joy.

## #6. "Dande-Mill"

*Procedure:*

In the fall when dandelions have turned white and children have engaged in the fun of sending the seeds flying through the air, provide this art project for the children.

Give each child a sheet of construction paper on which he either draws the stem and leaves of a dandelion, or cuts out one that you have duplicated and glues it on the paper. The children now cut out a pinwheel. It will probably be better for you to duplicate this on white construction paper so it will be easier for the children to cut the slits in the proper places. With help from parents or older students, attach the pinwheel to the paper at the top of the dandelion stem, using paper brads. The children can now blow on them as they did the dandelion seeds.

Do the same in the spring, but use yellow to make the pin-wheels as the dandelions are in bloom then.

### #7. "Reaching Conclusions"

*Objectives.*

1. To promote listening skills.
2. To review word meanings.
3. To develop language skills.
4. To enjoy participation.

*Procedure:*

If you like to create stories, you will enjoy using this activity while promoting word meanings and language usage.

By using the names of your students, which will instantly bring them to full attention, and by using some of the words the children learned on their autumn word trip, make up short stories to which the children must supply the conclusions. The following example has two places where you might stop the story and allow the children to supply the conclusion.

"Last Saturday, Joe, Robert, Peter, and David went to the park that is near a big forest. The boys were caught up in the excitement of kicking through the browning, rustling leaves and trying to catch the swirling leaves that were being caught up by the wind.

"They kept running through the crunchy leaves, getting closer and closer to the big woods. Suddenly, they heard the cracking sounds of twigs coming from the forest. Joe said, 'What's that?' 'I don't know, but I think it's time we got out of here.' said Robbie.

"Just then, they heard more sounds of crunching leaves and snapping twigs. Without waiting to find out any more, the boys started running. After going a short way, they looked back over their shoulder and . . . what do you think they saw?"

Let the children provide a conclusion here or you may go on with the story.

"Mary and her friend Betsy, the twins Jean and Bobby, and their friends Terri and Jimmy were coming out of the woods."

The children now supply their own conclusions. Any idea is acceptable if it is related to the story and if it follows in a logical sequence.

Make up similar stories for the other seasons.

### #9. "I'm a Little Apple Tree" (Douglas and Gloria Evans)

*Objectives:*

1. To remind the children that fall is the time when food is gathered for people as well as for animals.
2. To reinforce the concept that everything needs some special care.
3. To enjoy a creative activity song.

*Procedure:*

During the unit on the fall season, play this recording for the children to perform. This is a good time to remind them that they too should always stand and sit tall and straight. Follow this with the next activity.

### #10. "Nut Shell Prints"

*Objectives:*

1. To use materials collected.
2. To enjoy an art activity.
3. To create an apple tree like the one the children sang about in the preceding exercise.

*Procedure:*

If the children were able to find some nut shells or burrs on the trip, or have brought some to school that they have found, give each child a large sheet of construction paper and let each paint a large apple tree with water colors. Have red tempera paint ready when the tree is completed so the children can touch the inner edges of the broken shells in a shallow container of paint and make apples on their trees. If nut shells are not available, let the children use bottle caps to make the printed apples.

#### #11. "Apple Jelly"

*Objectives:*

1. To show the children one thing that can be done with apples besides eating them.
2. To introduce them to language terms.
3. To make a product that is edible.
4. To have something that they can take home for Thanksgiving.

*Procedure:*

When the apples get ripe in the fall, if you or any of the children have trees with apples, cook enough to make one batch of jelly. Strain the juice and take it to school. On a hotplate at school, cook the jelly and discuss the procedure with the children. Fill a small baby food jar (collected beforehand) for each child to take home for Thanksgiving. If it is a while until Thanksgiving, cover the jelly with paraffin, explaining this process and the reason for using it. After the jars are filled, there should be enough left over for the class to have some to eat with crackers. The foam part skimmed off the top is perfectly good jelly. Save this and any leftover jelly; pour into empty margarine tubs and allow to cool. It will be ready the next day for the children to eat.

If you wish, you may cook the apples at school, strain the juice off, and allow the children to eat the applesauce that is made in the process.

When fall grapes are picked, you can make jelly with them also. If no grapes are available, the unsweetened juice bought in stores makes very good jelly.

## #12. "Roasting Seeds"

*Objectives for procedures 12-14:*

1. To reinforce the idea that food comes from many unusual sources.
2. To introduce the children to the process of roasting.
3. To have pleasant, nourishing food to eat.

*Procedure:*

When sunflower seeds must be picked, save some to take to school, or ask the children to bring some that they have harvested. At Halloween, when you show the children how to cut and clean out the pumpkin to make jack-o'-lanterns, scrape out the seeds and allow to dry. If you live where peanuts are grown, bring some of them to school too.

These seeds should be dry enough to roast by the latter part of November. Bring a portable oven, or if you can borrow one from a parent, have her bring it to school to help you roast the nuts at school. Afterwards, the children may eat them.

Be sure to save some of the unroasted sunflower seeds for planting in the spring. Explain this to the children as you store them in a cupboard.

All of the seed plants that are gathered in the fall, such as pumpkin, sunflower, bean, pea, corn, etc., make lovely collage pictures at any time of the year.

## #13. "Peanut Butter"

*Procedure:*

Give the children some peanuts to hull. This will provide a coordination exercise and show them what is necessary in the process of making peanut butter. After the peanuts are hulled and roasted, grind them in a meat grinder, using the plate with the smallest holes. All of these steps should be done at school so the children can gain from the experience. Add a little peanut oil and salt to the ground nuts, stir, and let the children eat the peanut butter on crackers.

## #14. "Peanut Fudge"

*Procedure:*

Make some peanut fudge at school for Christmas treats. The children may eat some, and each child will put some in a container, made during an art period, to take home to his parents for a Christmas present. The following fudge recipe is a very old one, and it is very good as well as reliable:

In a saucepan put:

2 cups sugar
2 tablespoons of cocoa
1/2 cup syrup (do not use pancake syrup)
3/4 cup milk
pinch of salt

Add the milk slowly to the other ingredients, stirring to mix the cocoa. Cook over medium heat until mixture reaches a medium hard-ball stage. This will occur shortly after soft-ball stage. Add:

2 tablespoons margarine
2 teaspoons vanilla flavoring
1 cup roasted peanuts

Beat the mixture until it begins to harden. (If this seems to be taking a long time, set the pan in some cold water, stirring continually.) Pour onto a greased cookie sheet and allow to harden. It hardens quickly if it is cooked long enough.

## On the Inside Looking Out at the Wintry Conditions

## #15. "I Lost It (Them)"

*Objectives:*

1. To review a unit of study.
2. To reinforce science language skills.
3. To enjoy games, songs, and art projects.

*Procedure:*

Refer to "Mary's Lost Lamb" in Chapter 8. This game is

similar, except the children may use anything connected with a unit. For instance, if the unit being reviewed is winter, you might begin the game by saying, "I lost them. Will you help me find them?" The children reply with, "What are they like?" You might answer with:

"They are cold.
They are white.
There are lots of them.
They come from the sky.
Not one is like another.
They cover the ground.
We can make something with them."

Of course, the children will probably answer after three or four clues. Remind the children to use prominent clues last. The person who guesses the riddle first can be the next to tell his riddle.

The same idea is appropriate for any unit being studied.

### #16. "How Many Snowflakes" (Lucille Wood and Louise Scott)

*Procedure:*

To emphasize the snowflake in the preceding activity, play this recording either before or after that game. If you play it before, you may want to immediately follow it with your riddle in order to emphasize to the children, the procedure they are to use in telling their riddles. The children should act out the suggested actions in the song. This will remind them that sometimes it snows only a little and it melts immediately. It also reminds them that snow that hits our skin melts. Ask the children why this is so.

### #17. "Making Snowflakes"

*Procedure:*

Kindergarteners need an easy way to make snowflakes. Even though they can learn to do the folded ones, this one is very simple, and they can have success without your guidance once they have learned how.

Give each child a sheet of blue or black construction paper and a straw. On each table, place a small container of thin white paint. Tell the children to touch their straw slightly to the white paint so that only a tiny amount adheres. They then hold this over their construction paper and blow straight down from a distance of four to six inches. This gives a small splatter of "snow." If the children get too much paint on their straws, they will have globs instead of little pronged splatters.

Let the snowflakes dry until the following day. Give them back to the children and tell them that "it has been snowing all night" and now they can make a snowman. Out of white construction paper, they cut round circles and glue a snowman to their snow picture, adding any details they wish.

The same process can be used to make raindrops, except the paint should be a light blue.

## How to Have Fun in the Spring with Science Activities

### #18. "Egg, Tadpole, Frog"

*Objectives for 18-20:*

1. To gather frog eggs.
2. To raise tadpoles.
3. To watch tadpoles develop into frogs.
4. To learn by doing.
5. To improve science language skills.

*Procedure:*

If you live near water at all, you should be able to find a small stream where frogs lay their eggs. If you do not know of a place, ask some third-grade boys. They always seem to know. If possible, take the class to the place where the eggs are, and let them watch as you gather some. Put the eggs in a large, wide-mouthed jar with some of the weeds that are growing in that stream. When water is changed during the growing process, it is best to get it at this same location.

If you have an aquarium, put the frog eggs in it. If not, watch them closely as they will all hatch at about the same time, and a gallon jar is not large enough for all of the tadpoles to survive. There is not enough oxygen for the amount of tadpoles that will hatch. Even though you think you only have a few eggs, you may have nearly a hundred tadpoles.

Feed the tadpoles a dab of cooked oatmeal. Bring a small amount to school and put it in the refrigerator. It can be used a long time. Some people say to use fish food, but I have always raised my tadpoles on oatmeal.

If it looks as if all the tadpoles will live, give all but three away to other teachers or to children whose parents agree that they may bring them home.

When the tadpole is sprouting legs, he does not eat. He is absorbing his tail. When the frog emerges, put it in a container in which he can get out of the water when necessary. But do not make the mistake I did once. I put one in a turtle dish with sides about three inches high. The dish was fine, and since the frog was so tiny, it did not appear he could jump out. Well, he did. And he made his way to the nearest pool of water outside. That was where he was traced. How he got out of the house no one ever knew. Naturally, he was left in his new surroundings. But should you want to watch any further growth after the legs are formed, be sure the sides of the container are high enough so he cannot jump out.


#19. "Three Polliwogs" (Lucille Wood and Louise Scott)

*Procedure:*

Play this recording after the frog eggs have turned into tadpoles, and let the children learn the words so they can sing it often during the frog-growing process. The children should learn to dramatize the actions as they sing this cute song.

**#20. "Jumping Frogs"**
(by Hap Palmer, from *Pretend* by Educational Activities, Inc.)

*Procedure:*

This lovely little song allows the children to learn about the tadpole's life when he becomes a frog. The children perform the actions and dramatize the behavior of the frog as they sing the song.

**#21. "Scrappy Frog"**

*Objectives:*

1. To continue the study of the nature of frogs and other amphibians.
2. To enjoy an art project.
3. To develop coordination.

*Procedure:*

With the help of older students, tear many small pieces of green construction paper. They will be even more effective for this torn-paper collage if there are two or three shades of green intermixed in each batch.

On a master set, draw a frog that is at least four or five inches high. Let each child cut out his own frog. Write the children's names on the back, as this project will take more than one day.

Cover each table with newspapers; put a quantity of the torn pieces on each table; give each child a small paint brush, and put glue on each table. Show the children how to dab the brush lightly in the glue and apply a small amount to each piece of paper.

The children must cover the entire frog by overlapping each piece over another a tiny bit. When completely covered, give each child two buttons to glue on for the eyes. They should draw a line for the mouth with a felt marking pen or black crayon. These may be used for borders around bulletin boards.

Turtles are very pretty when done this way, but you need to let the children use a black crayon or felt marker to trace between each piece of paper in order to give the effect of the designs on a turtle shell. The paper pieces should be a variety of light browns. Snakes and other reptiles can be done in the same way.

**#22. "Little Ants"** (Hap Palmer)

*Objectives:*

1. To learn of the habits of ants.
2. To enjoy an activity song.
3. To stimulate science language skills.

*Procedure:*

In the spring, when ants start building their homes and inquisitive kindergarteners start asking questions, play this activity song as the class explores the role of ants and other insects.

As a follow-up, let the children make ants out of paper egg cartons. Each child will need only two spaces of a carton—each carton will make enough for six. These will be painted brown. Add eyes and antennae to finish the ant.

## Using the Calendar to Learn About Spring

Using the calendar should be a part of every day's beginning exercises. Counting, saying the days of the week, and learning about the different months are all important educational concepts. The activities included here are an extension of the daily routine.

**#23. "Lion or Lamb"**

*Objectives for procedures 23-24:*

1. To stimulate awareness for weather conditions.
2. To introduce old folk sayings.

3. To provide counting experiences through the calendar.

*Procedure:*

In order to see if the saying about March winds is true every time, draw several lion's and lamb's heads to use on your calendar. They should be the size that will fit your calendar spaces. When one is added to the calendar, a number can be written on it to signify the date.

Tell the children the saying, "If the month of March comes in like a lion, it will go out as a lamb," and vice versa. They should tell you each day if the wind is gentle and calm or blowing. The calendar is made up each day after the children arrive. At the end of the month, everyone will be able to see if the saying was true or not. The days for each type of weather should be counted to see if there were more windy days than calm ones.

## #24. "April Showers"

*Procedure:*

To emphasize the saying that "April showers bring May flowers," cut out several umbrellas that will fit your calendar spaces. Also, cut suns and clouds for sunny and cloudy days. If it is partly cloudy, put up a sun partly obscured by the clouds. At the end of the month, count the number of days of each kind of weather. On one of the cloudy days do the following exercise.

## #25. "Little Clouds" (Douglas and Gloria Evans)

*Objectives:*

1. To emphasize sky conditions.
2. To enjoy an activity song.
3. To improve coordination.

*Procedure:*

While out for a walk in the spring, when there are lots of white clouds, ask the children to sit down on the grass and look at the clouds floating by. Explain to them why the clouds are moving and ask them to look at the clouds to see if they can find any forms that look like something to them. Soon the children will be finding all types of different forms.

Perform the "Little Clouds" activity song when you get back to the classroom. Tell the children to close their eyes and pretend they are sitting on one of the clouds looking down on the earth.

As a follow-up, give each child a sheet of blue construction paper, glue, and cotton balls or quilt batting, and let them produce a picture with white clouds in it.

**#26. "Whirlwind"** (Lucille Wood and Louise Scott)

*Objectives:*

1. To emphasize weather conditions caused by hot and cold air currents.
2. To promote science language skills.
3. To enjoy an activity song and art project while learning.

*Procedure:*

In the late spring or early summer, depending on your climate, show the children the whirlwinds that are prevalent. Explain to them the reason for these and play this activity recording as the children perform the actions of a whirlwind.

Follow this recording with this art project. Let the children paint an outdoor scene with water colors. Emphasize that you want an entire scene with houses, people, plants, etc. When this is completed, give the children some brown paint which you have toned down with white to make a light tan, and have them make a whirlwind somewhere on their picture. Ask the children why a house will get dusty after a whirlwind, even though it has been thoroughly cleaned. This will help them understand why parents must clean house so often.

Scientific exploration begins when we are born. Build upon

the information that the children have already gleaned from their environment and add information that will enlighten the concepts the children have acquired. By building on these simple concepts, the foundation is laid for future scientific exploration. The foundation you build is very important!

# 10

## Involving Kindergarteners in Their Health and Safety

### Why Involving Kindergarteners in Their Physical Well-Being Is Important

Parents find out early in their children's lives that regardless of how much they watch their little ones, they cannot possibly watch these naturally curious youngsters every second of the day. Therefore, training begins as warnings—warnings of dangers involved in actions performed without regard to the possible serious consequences. This is why health and safety training is a must at school as well as at home. Children must learn early in life that certain consequences occur if they do not follow prescribed precautions. They must eventually accept some of the responsibility for their own safe conduct and healthy living. Mother or teacher cannot always be around to tell them to "put on a coat or cap" or to "look carefully before crossing a street."

Your role as the kindergarten teacher is to continue with the training that the children have already learned at home and to carry this training one step further. You should now involve the child in his responsibility for his safety and health as it affects the community.

## Developing Self-Help Attributes

It is not easy to teach young children to take the responsibility for their own health and safety. The best approach is to let the children know that you expect them to take care of themselves.

### #1. "I Can Do It Myself"

*Objectives:*

1. To develop each child's ability to take responsibility for his minor wounds.
2. To encourage self-reliance.
3. To teach the proper way to take care of certain minor wounds.

*Procedure:*

Very early in my career, an astute and understanding mother told me of a child's malady, stating, "He has been taught to take care of it himself. I only wanted you to be aware of it."

Subsequent events proved her to be correct. He would always answer a request to help by saying, "I can do it myself." Then why not others? Their little everyday scratches and bruises were nothing compared to this boy's serious medical problem.

Afterwards, I made it one of the objectives that I checked each time I sent home child appraisal lists. The item read:

"Cleans and takes care of own small cuts and scratches."

This is not done in disregard for a child's health. On the contrary, it is to be made into a learning process. When a child is hurt, he reports to the teacher. Most injuries are very insignificant and very slight anyway. These children are then taught to wash and clean the area very well. If a child has a wound that needs a bandage, show him how to apply it without touching the wound. If he has a bleeding wound, he should be sent to the nurse.

Children should be praised for their ability to take responsibility for the scratches that come along and for taking care of them. One way to do this is to have a picture of a nurse or doctor, or both, on the bulletin board; then, when some child is very brave about an incident and takes care of the minor ones in the proper way, his name is written on a card and put on the bulletin board. The bulletin board could be entitled: "Our Brave Doctors and Nurses."

Kindergarteners are not too young to be taught to take care of minor incidents if they are properly supervised. They learn to accept this as the proper and expected thing to do. But they also know when a wound needs extra care. This is very important too—to know when "I need your help" is necessary.

### Learning to Understand Our Need for Good Health and Safe Conduct Through Pantomime

#### #2. "Pantomiming Community Helpers"

*Objectives for procedures 2-4:*

1. To understand the role of our health and safety helpers.
2. To improve the children's attitude towards health and safety helpers.
3. To improve desires to take care of, and be responsible for, our own health and safety.
4. To improve the mental and emotional attitudes towards unpleasant health precautions.

*Procedure:*

During and following a unit on the community helpers involved in our personal health and safety, let the children get together in small groups with parent or student helpers to decide how they will pantomime a specific helper. Assign each group a different person to portray, such as a doctor, dentist, nurse, policeman, fireman, ambulance attendant, etc. When the children are ready, let each group perform before the others until someone in the audience guesses. Remind helpers that students should learn to be subtle at first and save revealing characteristics until last. If not, the children will readily guess who they are representing.

### #3. "Pantomiming Danger"

*Procedure:*

Do the same type of pantomime procedure with dangers that can threaten the lives of children. Some examples are:

1. Drinking poisonous liquid from bottles
2. Taking pills and medicines
3. Playing with matches
4. Chewing leaves and berries from poisonous plants
5. Running with sharp objects in hands or mouths
6. Swimming without adult supervision
7. Sticking objects in the nose or ears
8. Eating sweets
9. Running into streets behind parked cars.
10. Going outside without a coat or raincoat on cold and wet days.
11. Sticking metal objects in electrical outlets
12. Standing up in a moving car
13. Watching television with no exercise
14. Jaywalking

Ask your helpers to have their small groups emphasize the results that can happen if the negative attribute is carried out in real life. Acting out something of this nature helps the children remember the positive rules much more easily.

## #4. "Pantomiming Health and Safety Rules"

*Procedure:*

Following the preceding pantomiming exercises which could take several days, give the children the opportunity to pantomime the reverse situations. As the children act out the proper way to follow good rules in their daily living, they are actually reminding themselves that "this is the way I can stay happy and healthy."

## Music and Art Projects That Emphasize Proper Living Habits

Although I am again sending you outside this book to obtain materials with which to do these exercises, these wonderful, exciting recordings involve the children in active participation in their learning. The following recordings are from Hap Palmer's album, *Learning Basic Skills Through Music—Health and Safety* (Educational Activities, Inc.).

*Objectives for procedures 5-13:*

1. To reinforce rules that have been presented in connection with health and safety.
2. To enjoy exciting words and music while performing the actions of the good rules that the words teach.
3. To develop coordination.

## #5. "Take a Bath"

*Procedure:*

This is a fantastic little activity song. When the bathing procedures are carried out during the song, the children learn the proper elements of a bath and why it is important they stay clean.

Follow this song with an art project. Give each child a sheet of colored construction paper. Out of other scraps, the children are to cut a bathtub and glue on the construction paper. Next, they cut out a drawing of a child and slide it behind the tub. They may add any other features they wish to the picture.

## #6. "Buckle Your Seat Belt"

*Procedure:*

This is excellent for teaching an important safety precaution. It should be played over and over during the year. The children love its rhythmic music and words, and the valuable lesson is apparent from the name of the selection.

Following the song, have the children fold a piece of paper in half. On one side they draw a picture of people wearing seat belts, and on the other they draw a picture of what could happen if there was an accident and the occupants did not have on their safety belts.

## #7. "Posture Exercises" and "Exercise Every Day"

*Procedure:*

Both of these songs emphasize the need for exercising the body every day. The activities that follow along with the words allow the children to engage in some good exercises while enjoying exhilarating musical selections.

Following the exercises, give each child a sheet of paper on which he can either draw or cut out of scrap paper, a picture of a rocket (mentioned in one of the songs) and a child who is standing beside the rocket as straight and tall as possible trying to touch the sky. This will remind the children that sitting and standing tall and straight is the way we have good posture when we grow up.

## #8. "Keep the Germs Away"

*Procedure:*

This example is an extension of Activity #5 in this chapter. After the children take baths, they must continue to keep themselves neat and clean, and they must take care of their hair, teeth, nails, etc., every day.

When the children finish this selection, let them pantomime the activities and what happens if we do not stay clean. As the song suggests, people do not like to be around us when we do not smell clean. The positive side should also be portrayed.

### #9. "Safe Way"

*Procedure:*

Before the children do this exercise, have posters ready that show the results of the inappropriate actions on the part of people who do not follow rules of fire, water, and bicycle safety. Remind the children after the selection that having fun involves using safety measures.

After the selection, have one group dramatize the selection for handling fire; another group will dramatize water safety; the last group will dramatize bicycle safety. Later, you may also want each group to draw pictures that relate the story of their dramatization.

### #10. "Brush Away"

*Procedure:*

This selection and some of the others just mentioned have already been suggested in the chapter on music, but all are special enough to be mentioned again in this chapter. Since brushing teeth is so easy for children to "forget," reminding them as often as possible is important.

As was suggested in Activity #1 in this chapter, dentists of the week would be appropriate when emphasizing the need to keep teeth clean. Add a picture of a dentist to the nurse and doctor pictures on the bulletin board. Ask each child each day if he brushed his teeth last night and this morning. Put the names of those who brushed under the picture of the dentist as "dentist's helpers." You will have to take their word as to whether they brushed their teeth or not.

## #11. "Cover Your Mouth"

*Procedure:*

This selection has also been mentioned, but its importance can never be overemphasized. Too many colds are spread because of poor judgment.

When this selection has been learned, have the children select a partner. One child will be the mother; the other will be the child who has a cold and must stay in bed. As the song is being played again, the mother hands the child a tissue to cover his mouth. As he lays in bed, the mother is taking his temperature and giving him fluids to drink. Change the roles of the partners so each gets a turn to play each role.

## #12. "Alice's Restaurant"

*Procedure:*

This song emphasizes all the proper foods that children should eat each day. When the selection has been sung and the actions have been portrayed, give each child a sheet of paper that has been pre-folded in fourths, on which they can draw or paint pictures of these four food groups.

## #13. "Stop, Look and Listen"

*Procedure:*

We can never overemphasize proper care in walking across streets or playing near streets. Children just do not seem to understand that those same cars that take us to nice places can also destroy or cripple us. Perhaps a better way to look at it is that children expect grown-ups to watch out for them because someone always has. This is why we must stress the importance of children accepting the responsibility for their own safety as soon as possible. Follow this activity with the next two exercises.

## Effective Ways to Strengthen Perceptual Qualities

**#14. "Careful Observation"**

*Objectives for procedures 14-15:*

1. To emphasize the need for carefully observing the surroundings before acting.
2. To reinforce safety concepts.
3. To emphasize how little we actually see of our environment.

*Procedure:*

When teaching the children to stop, look, and listen at all corners before crossing streets, try this experiment to show them how we often look without actually perceiving what's around us.

On a bulletin board that is near to where all the children are generally located, place several safety pictures. These can be related to any aspect of safety, not just to traffic. Be sure the pictures are colorful and are of the type that generally comand the attention of the children. However, do not mention them to the children. If someone makes a comment, make appropriate remarks, but say no more.

At the end of about four days, take the pictures down. The following day, ask the children to tell you all about what they saw on that particular bulletin board for the past few days. Some will be able to tell you a few things, while others will remember none.

When they finish, tell them that this was an experiment to show them how careless we are sometimes about looking. Sometimes we get to corners and think we look, but after a quick glance we rush out into the street.

Put up the pictures again, one by one, and discuss them. When you have finished, ask the children if they know now why it is particularly important that we really look before we do something rash. This could be running into a street, drinking from a bottle without looking at the label, running without looking where you are going, going into deep water, and so on.

## #15. "Careful Listening"

*Procedure:*

Do the same activity with sounds. There are recordings on the market that have all sorts of sounds on them. Two of these are: *Sounds of Animals,* recorded by Arthur M. Greenhall, Folkways Records, and *Wild Animal Safari* by James Ramey, LeCrone Teaching Aids. Or, you can make your own recordings by carrying around your tape recorder for a few days.

Let the children listen to the recording the first time, without telling them why. When it has finished, ask the children to tell you the sounds they heard. Most children will remember only very prominent sounds.

Play the recording again each day for several days. At the end of each playing, the children will be able to tell you more and more sounds they heard because they now are aware that this is the purpose.

Remind the children that they have the same responsibility when crossing the street. They must actually listen to know if a car is coming.

This exercise is good to use for sound perception at any time.

## Games That Reinforce Health and Safety Practices

## #16. "Help"

*Objectives for procedures 16-18:*

1. To reinforce acts of health and safety.
2. To improve coordination.
3. To emphasize good health and safety habits.

*Procedure:*

Approximately one third of the children should make a large circle, with 4 or '5 ft. between each child. These students will be the saving agents. Two or three of the other students will stand several feet behind this circle. They are the enemy. The rest of the children will be seated in the middle of the circle. They are playing what they are—children. They must run to one of the community helpers that help us when we have specific problems. Some possibilities for enemies and the saving agents are:

| Enemy | Saving Agent |
|-------|--------------|
| Fire | Firemen or Forest Rangers |
| Drowning | Lifeguard |
| Measles | Doctor |
| Cuts | Nurse |
| Cavities | Dentist |

Suppose the enemy is Measles. The children who are the doctors are in the large circle. The children who portray themselves are seated inside the circle. You then call, "The enemy, Measles, is coming." The children in the center should get up and try to get to one of the doctors before the enemy can catch them. If the enemy catches any of the children, they must become part of the enemy and help catch the others.

Reverse the roles each group is playing in order for the children to play all the roles.

### #17. "Fire"

*Procedure:*

On two large boxes draw a scene of an apartment building on fire. Cut out some of the windows for the children to throw their beanbags through. The beanbags are going to take the place of the water that firemen use.

Divide the children into two groups. Set the boxes about six to ten feet from the children. Each team now lines up behind a line marked in some way. Each child has a beanbag. As the first child throws his beanbag, he steps out of the way for the second, and so on. Each child tries to get his beanbag through a window into the apartment house. When the children for both teams have finished, count to see how many beanbags are in each box. The one with the most beanbags has won.

Each team may name themselves before starting, if they wish. One team may want to be Station 97, while the other wants to be Station 16. The two stations are having a race to see who can put out a fire in an old building used for practice purposes. Explain to the children the reason for having practice sessions.

#### #18. "The Bad Cold"

*Procedure:*

This game is played to emphasize how easy it is to spread our germs and diseases to others. One child is chosen to be the one who has a bad cold (or other disease). The other children sit on the floor in no particular order. When the game starts, all the children must stand. The child with the bad cold tries to tag another child before he can sit down again. When a child sits down to keep from getting caught, he must get up again as soon as possible. As children are tagged, they now have a bad cold and must help tag the others. When all the children have been tagged, select a new child to be the one with the cold.

By building on the foundation laid by parents, you provide meaningful experiences and motivating activities to impress upon the children the necessity for certain do's and don'ts in healthy and safe living.

The experiences that we provide to our kindergarteners becomes the cornerstone for their future growth and development. Of course, this applies to all areas, not only to health and safety. This is why our task is so tremendously important. Just think how important you are!

# 11

## Emphasizing Emotional Needs Through Self-Knowledge and Concern for Others

### How Emotional Stability Relates to the Social Sciences

How do we separate emotions into one area of study? We cannot. Emotional security, or insecurity, reveals itself in reading, writing, math, health, or the social sciences.

Because our emotions are closely tied to the environment in which we live and learn, our social surroundings provide the best places to study the effects this environment has on children's lives—beginning first in the home, expanding into the schools and community, later into the state, and finally into the world. With the advent of television and the travel pattern of today's families, the social environment quickly takes on many different cultures.

As kindergarten teachers, we must teach children to accept others as the human beings that they are. They must learn that regardless of where a person lives in this world, he is not unlike ourselves. We are all alike since we all seek love, understanding, someone to love and care for, and we all wish desperately to be contributing members of our society.

Therefore, our prime objective in teaching the social sciences in kindergarten is to make children aware of, and to accept, their ever-expanding environment whether it is near or far away.

## Productive Ways to Teach Statistics About Oneself

Children are often separated from their parents in large, crowded areas. And some wander from their streets and get lost while trying to get home again. It is imperative, then, that every child in kindergarten be capable of telling someone where he lives and what his name and phone number are. If he can do this when lost, he will soon be returned to the security and protection of his home and family.

### #1. "Name, Address and Phone Number"

*Objectives:*

1. To teach children their full name, address, and phone number.
2. To reinforce this knowledge until every child can immediately respond with the information.
3. To make the children aware of ways to help themselves when necessary.

*Procedure:*

One of your first objectives at the beginning of every school year should be to have every child learn his full name, address, and phone number. Some will learn these very quickly; parents will work with some, and others will take a while. But eventually, every child will be equipped with the information necessary to get him back to his home if he should ever get lost.

It does take time to teach children these facts, but one easy way is to have each respond to the roll call each day with one piece of information. First, they should learn their full names. Call each by the first name, and the children respond with the complete name. When names are learned, work on addresses, then on telephone numbers. After the children have mastered these, they should be asked to repeat the information at least once a month for review purposes.

The following activities involve some more of the exciting recordings that so aptly teach vital statistics as a by-product.

**#2. "What Is Your Name?"**
(Hap Palmer, from the album *Learning Basic Skills Through Music*, Vol. I.)

*Objectives:*

1. To have fun while learning the name.
2. To reinforce first, middle, and last names independent of each other.

*Procedure:*

This recording reinforces the other methods you are using to teach children their names. Before the selection starts, tell the children to say only one part of their name when asked— either the first, middle, or the last name. Too few children would get to answer if each child told his entire name. Besides, children should be able to tell others only one part of their name. This is the fun way to learn how.

**#3. "My Name"**

*Objectives:*

1. To promote the learning of the name.
2. To give a reward for information learned.

*Procedure:*

When you start teaching the children their names, make a colorful tag for each child with his full name written on it. The tags will be even more attractive if you use shapes such as fish, birds, fruit, animal heads, etc., as designs on which to write the names. Place these tags on a bulletin board. When the children are consistently able to repeat their full names and can tell you their first, middle, and last names individually, give the tags to the children to wear home.

The children love to receive these little awards, and it often gives them the incentive needed to learn factual information quickly.


### #4. "My Address"

*Objectives:*

1. To promote the learning of the address.

2. To give an award for information learned.

3. To learn why maps are important.

*Procedure:*

If you live in a city that has a large street map, get one and put it on a bulletin board. Around this map, place rectangles representing doors of houses. On each door, write the address of a child. Place a pin, with a string attached, at the street location of each child's house. Attach the string to the corresponding address on a door. Explain the map and the location of each child's house in relation to the school site.

Around the map, place different colored construction paper houses on which you have drawn in windows and other simple features with a felt marker. Do not draw in a door shape. When the children can repeat their addresses consistently, take the door from the map and glue it on the houses. The children may then take them home.

If there is no city map, put the doors in the center of the bulletin board with houses placed around them. Add the doors to the houses as the children learn their addresses.

### #5. "My Telephone Number"

*Objectives:*

1. To promote the learning of the phone number.

2. To reward the children for information learned.

*Procedure:*

Follow the same procedure as in the previous two suggestions, except put the phone number of each child on a telephone cut from different bright colored construction paper. Arrange these around a large telephone in the center of a bulletin board on which you have written, "I Know My Phone Number."

## Promoting Emotional Adjustment Through Music, Art, and Dramatization

Through the active involvement in musical selections that are exhilarating, and in art and dramatic exercises that elaborate on what has been taught, children cannot help but learn to understand themselves and others better. Again, consider the recordings that are used here as part of your future kindergarten supply needs. They are excellent for so many special teaching situations.

### #6. "Feelings" and "What Do People Do?" (Hap Palmer)

*Objectives for procedures 6-10:*

1. To help the children understand that their negative feelings are not uncommon or unnatural.
2. To encourage children to feel better about themselves.
3. To enjoy activity songs that teach about emotions.
4. To enjoy art and drama activities.

*Procedure:*

Play these two recordings as the children act out the different expressions. Remind the children that we all have the same negative feelings at times and they are natural responses to discouragement, anger, fear, and frustration. However, as we grow older, we are expected to improve our reactions to unhappy situations by controlling ourselves and accepting the rights that others have.

Follow the music period with an art project. Give each child a sheet of paper pre-folded in half. Ask each table of children to illustrate a different emotional situation. They will first draw the negative behavior on one side of the paper, then they will draw the positive change on the opposite side. The following illustration is given as the type of situation you can propose to the different groups.

> *Negative:* Jack is very angry at his father for not taking him to the store with him. He storms to his room, slams the door, and lays sulking on the bed.

> *Positive:* When Dad brings home a new bicycle for Jack's birthday, along with cake and ice cream, Jack apologizes to his dad for getting angry. He knew that Dad wanted to surprise him. He also knew that Dad would have taken him to the store if there had not been a good reason for doing otherwise.

Make up similar emotional situations for other reactions.

## #7. "Body Image"

*Procedure:*

There are several recordings that are developed especially to teach children their different body parts and how each child's body relates to the space around him. Some of these selections also help promote directional changes, left and right discrimination, and important terms needed in subject areas.

From Hap Palmer's album, *Getting to Know Myself:*

1. "Hello"
2. "Sammy"
3. "Touch"
4. "Shake Something"
5. "The Circle"
6. "Turn Around"
7. "Circle Game"

8. "Left and Right"

9. "Change"

10. "The Opposite"

From Young People's Records' album, *Me, Myself and I:*

"Counting Song"

After these selections have been played, have the children engage in the following art activities:

1. Draw and paint pictures of people with as many different body parts as the children are capable of drawing.

2. Trace around both hands and the feet on construction paper. When these are cut out, the children can arrange them in a design on a large sheet of construction paper.

3. At a time when you have several parent or student helpers, trace around each child's body, letting them fill in all details and add clothing. When the figures are cut out, they may be displayed for a time before the children take them home.

**#8. "Greetings"**

*Procedure:*

It is of utmost importance to kindergarten children that they fit into the scheme of things. They want to learn the names of other children and join in the fun that others are having. In other words, they want to be accepted.

Most children have few qualms about approaching a new child and asking him his name. This is why they get acquainted so quickly. Some of the musical selections that help with this task are:

1. "Hello" (Hap Palmer)

2. "Be My Friend" (Hap Palmer)

3. "Howdja Do" (An old song that can be found on different recordings.)

These fun songs and the activities associated with them help children enjoy themselves as they learn each other's names, learn to shake hands, and share a good time together.

Following this type of activity selection, give the children a problem to work. Ask them to give serious consideration to how they would communicate to others if they could not talk. Tell them of famous people such as Helen Keller who could not talk (and, in her case, could not hear) but, because of their persistence, learned to cope with a speaking society.

When the children have thought about this for a few minutes, have groups of three or four children meet with you and parent or student helpers to decide how they can pantomime a greeting to the other students. Follow the dramatization with the following selection.

### #9. "The Teacher Who Couldn't Talk" (Hap Palmer)

*Procedure:*

This is an exciting recording which treats the mute factor and also promotes acquaintance with different musical instruments. The children are actively involved with the delightful activities that the instruments "tell" them to perform. After this selection, ask the children what kind of teacher they think this lady would be if she were their teacher. Undoubtedly, they will all say they would like to have her for a teacher. This and the previous activity will be good examples to use in the study of sign language during Indian units.

### #10. "Rushing" (Hap Palmer)

*Procedure:*

Children need to know that parents are often in a hurry because they have jobs that must be done in order to take care of the family. When people in a family are rushed, the tensions and emotional levels are high. Children often feel the brunt of these tensions, even though unintentionally.

When this recording is being played, explain to the children why rushing can become an emotional experience for everyone. Perhaps, if this recording is played often enough, the children will understand the "why" of certain emotional occurrences within their households.

## Using Holidays of Other Lands to Learn About Other Cultures

Holidays are special to everyone. When children learn about others through the special days other people enjoy, they are able to relate to them although cultural differences may be great. Teaching kindergarteners about children in other lands through their holidays is one of the best ways to train the youngsters to accept all racial and cultural differences.

### #11. "Special Days in Other Lands"

*Objectives:*

1. To teach children about other cultures.
2. To promote goodwill for other people.
3. To enjoy a profitable study.

*Procedure:*

During December, when Christmas is so prevalent in the minds of children, discussing with them, showing them pictures and films, and learning about the holidays that children in other lands enjoy, have always stimulated my kindergarteners. They remember the other children and their respective countries by the exciting things they do in their countries. My students would often bring up these comparisons weeks, and even months, later.

The following are some study suggestions:

1. The David C. Cook Publishing Co. has a packet of pictures entitled, *Children of Other Lands*. It contains stories about the children and suggestions for the

teacher. However, not enough holidays are included, so you will need to supplement the ideas in this packet with some of the following suggestions.

2. Find materials for holidays in other countries in the library.

3. Dolls from other countries signifying the race and style of dress are very effective in teaching about a country.

4. Carrying out some of the customs for a day at school is another effective way to enhance the study of other children. For instance, a Doll's Day for girls and a Kite Day for boys would be especially productive and exciting when learning about the special days of Japan.

5. End the unit with a Mexican Christmas and the breaking of a piñata. This gives the children an exciting climax to their study of other holidays.

This chapter has been concerned with how a child feels about himself and how he relates to others who enter his environment. If you are able to instill the acceptance of any, and all, cultural differences that exist in our world, the task will be done well.

# 12

## Developing Perceptual Skills— The Prime Objective of the Kindergarten Curriculum

### Key Roles Perceptual Skills Play in the Kindergarten Curriculum

It is only through the use of the five senses—with which most children are endowed—that real learning takes place. Knowledge is achieved when the five senses have become so closely integrated that there is no longer any real division between one sense and another. This is why coordination skills are the prime prerequisites of any kindergarten program. The activities that we use to teach kindergarteners must be purposely attuned to the training of the senses in such a way that one sense becomes an integral part of another in the learning process.

Thus, we can say that anything we do in kindergarten is connected with, and must be based upon, being rooted in the development of the five senses—the perceptual keys of our bodies.

We cannot divorce the perceptual skills from coordination development, since the integration of all the perceptual skills *is* coordination at its highest level. Our aim in kindergarten is to guide children toward this high level of achievement in every area of the curriculum.

## Art Fun That Develops Tactile Perception

#1. "Macaroni and Spaghetti"

*Objectives:*

1. To develop tactile perception.
2. To develop visual-motor skills.
3. To develop the sense of smell.
4. To have fun with an unusual art medium.

*Procedure:*

Cook macaroni and spaghetti until almost done. Take it to school and let the children make outlines of objects on their backgrounds of watercolor or finger painting. If you will add food coloring to it, it can be used on white construction paper without a background.

Some children will resist using it at first because of its feel, but they will soon join in the fun with the others. They should lay it on their paper in the pattern they want, then pick it up piece by piece and, using a small paint brush, brush a little glue where each piece is to lay. Allow the projects to dry until the macaroni and spaghetti has hardened.

Of course, children can also work with macaroni and spaghetti that is uncooked. It does not stay on the paper as well, since the cooked material has a paste all its own. The tactile experience is not as pronounced with the dried food.

Numerals and letters can be easily made with the spaghetti. Sets for the numerals and objects for the letter sounds can also be quickly made from the cooked spaghetti, since it can readily be bent into any shape.

## #2. "Finger Painting"

*Objectives:*

1. To enjoy an art project that will develop tactile perception.
2. To learn to use the hands in creating pleasing art.
3. To develop visual-motor skills.

*Procedure:*

When children come to kindergarten, they are introduced to paint brushes and easel painting, often for the first time in their lives. The hand has not fully developed in coordination at this period in children's lives. Adding the paint brush, which now becomes an extension of the hand, compounds the coordination problem. Of course, the children should learn to use it, but would it not make more sense to teach a child to first use his fingers in painting? This is not finger painting as we think of it, although it is certainly included. This type of finger painting is just that—using the finger, or fingers, with which to paint.

Give every child a piece of paper when introducing this. One color of paint (not too thin) in shallow containers on a well-covered table is all that is necessary. Now show the children how to make long strokes, short strokes, swirling strokes, prints, etc., as they put their fingers in the paint and put it on their paper. Just think how easy it would be for every child to go home with a lovely flower or tree made with simple finger strokes under your guidance. Try it! You will be surprised, and the children will love it.

Of course, finger painting as we generally know it is a must in kindergarten. Try the following activity when you need to cover a bulletin board.

## #3. "Finger Paint Backgrounds"

*Objectives:*

1. To develop visual-motor skills.
2. To develop tactile perception.
3. To obtain a background for a bulletin board.

*Procedure:*

Cut strips of butcher paper to fit a large bulletin board. Divide the larger pieces into four or five smaller ones so small groups can work on it. Mark the pieces for your own information in order to put the right colors on them, if you wish a specific scene. For instance, if it is an outdoor scene, you may want to use blues at the top, with some yellow added for sun rays. Greens, and possibly browns, will probably be used from the middle downward.

Put the paint with some liquid starch on each piece of paper and let small groups of children get on both sides of the paper to finger paint. The paint should first be spread out to cover the entire sheet of paper before the children add any designs.

This is an easy way to get a background, and it allows the children to develop skills at the same time. If you have an outside work area, finger painting outside can certainly save a lot of cleaning up afterwards.

## #4. "Pudding Painting"

*Objectives:*

1. To develop visual-motor skills.
2. To develop tactile and olfactory perceptions.
3. To discover the enjoyment of working with eatable substances.

*Procedure:*

Finger painting with paint is fun for youngsters, but add pudding and the children will get in a lot of extra "licks." Not all are on paper either, so you should be sure the children have clean hands when you start this; but, that's the joy of working with this substance.

Just think how easy it would be for children to remember how to make the letter *m* and the sound it makes if it were performed in the pudding with the final stroke ending in their mouth. The short vowel *o* is another one that would be especially easy to remember. Drawing these letters and sounds with an outline picture in the pudding is a great way to introduce factual information. Try it at least once with your students.

### #5. "Hand and Foot Prints"

*Objectives:*

1. To develop visual-motor skills.
2. To develop tactile perception.
3. To create an art project that can be used for a decoration.

*Procedure:*

Some day when you are finger painting, let the children transfer a painted hand to another sheet of clean paper. Be sure that names are on the paper ahead of time. Footprints can also be done in the same way, if you wish. However, you will need good washing facilities if you make footprints.

When the prints are dry, the children should cut them out very carefully and glue them with rubber cement to Styrofoam meat trays. A contrasting color should be glued to the inside to make a pleasing background before adding the prints. These may be taken home as gifts or to hang in the children's rooms.

#6. "Yarn Projects"

*Objectives:*

1. To develop visual-motor skills.
2. To develop tactile skills.
3. To develop a pleasing art product.
4. To learn factual material.

*Procedure:*

Yarn is an easy product with which to work on paper, and is even easier on cloth. With a thin line of glue under the yarn, it will adhere very quickly and easily—if the glue stays off the fingers! If each child has a wet paper towel on which to clean his hands before handling the yarn, it will be much easier to handle.

Complete scenes can be made with yarn as the outlining material. It can also be used to fill in small objects. A sun made with yarn wound repeatedly is only one example of this process.

Yarn adheres very well to cloth. Felt material cut out in the shape of stockings for Christmas, hearts for Valentines, flowers for spring, etc., can be decorated with yarn to make the product very lovely.

Yarn letters and numerals glued to construction paper make lovely art pictures. Short pieces of yarn cut into strips or rolled into circles can be added to numerals to show the number of the sets. Simple objects in an outlined form can be added to each letter to show the sound. These would make lovely booklets, with different bright colors of yarn used for the symbols.

Let each child cut a stencil from one of yours. (Using one of their own will keep the glue off of yours.) After the stencils are cut out, the children lay them on their paper, run a thin line of glue around them, lift up the stencils, and lay yarn on top of the glue. Several shapes from the same stencil can be placed in a design on a large sheet of construction paper. Overlapping one over the other in different colors of yarn would make a lovely design.

## #7. "Stringing Popcorn"

*Objectives for procedures 7-8:*

1. To develop tactile and olfactory perception.
2. To develop visual-motor skills.
3. To obtain a lovely decoration and stimulate the perception of taste at the same time.

*Procedure:*

Children love to be able to work with something that is pretty or good to eat. Stringing popcorn at Christmas is a perceptual exercise that involves every sense we have. With blunt-pointed needles, the children can string a small string of popcorn for the classroom tree or for other room decorations. The children can eat the corn that is left after stringing their piece.

Popping the corn in the classroom adds to the fun and excitement. The smells are heavenly, and the children love to hear and see the popcorn as it swells in the popper, if you have a container through which they can see.

## #8. "Stringing Snapdragons"

*Procedure:*

Although the children cannot eat the snapdragons, they certainly can enjoy the vivid colors and the fragrance of these lovely flowers. They are easy to string. When the flowers are opened, the needle penetrates the flower very little. Necklaces, bracelets, and belts can be made from these delightful flowers, if they grow where you live. Show the children how they open to make earrings without any work.

**#9. "Rickrack Art"**

*Objectives:*

1. To develop visual-motor skills.
2. To develop tactile skills.
3. To obtain a lovely finished product.

*Procedure:*

Cut small pieces of rickrack for each child and encourage everyone to create a figure with it. Show the children some examples that you have made. (See Figure 12-1 for some suggestions.) The creations that can be made from this item are only limited by the imagination of the artists. For instance, think of a dragon, worm, bee, bird, tree, flower, or maybe a "crooked house" for the "crooked man," a mountainous road, a bridle path, almost anything that one could think of would look lovely when made of some bright rickrack with extra features added

**Figure 12-1**

with felt markers. The children should first glue the piece to the construction paper before attempting any drawing.

Most people who sew would certainly have a few scraps that they would leave at school for the children to make art projects. Small pieces of lace or other trims can also make lovely additions to artwork.

## Examples of Activities That Develop
## Auditory Perception

### #10. "Echo"

*Objectives for procedures 10-12:*

1. To develop auditory perception.
2. To develop a sense of direction for sounds.
3. To develop precise sequential order.

*Procedure:*

Let one child go behind a screen or other object where the children cannot see him. Have this child say a short sentence. Call on one of the other children, who is to repeat the sentence in the exact order in which it was said. If he can "echo" the correct words in the proper sequence, he can become the speaker. Children must realize the need for clear and distinct enunciation in order for the other children to understand them. They will also have to listen very carefully in order to interpret what is said in the proper order.

If you have an aide or parent helper, divide your class in half, each half separated from the others by some divider. One child on one team says a short sentence. The children on the other team try to echo the correct statement and tell who the child was who said it. This takes on a second dimension of auditory discrimination.

When the children understand the idea and can play this game fairly well, have them make up nonsense sentences for the others to repeat.

Small groups working with a helper can be subdivided to play this game. This will be particularly beneficial with those children who are having difficulties with this type of activity.

## #11. "Sounds of Music"

*Procedure:*

One child places himself behind some object from which he cannot see the others. Quietly pick up a rhythm instrument and hand it to another child. This child plays it two or three times and hands it back to you. When the instrument is put away, the child who is hidden comes out and tells from which direction he heard the music and what instrument it was.

Have the children spread out all over the room for this activity so there is no crowding. If there is enough distance between each child, they should soon be able to pinpoint the youngster who played the instrument. When they become proficient at this, decrease the area in which the group is located.

## #12. "Sentence Order"

*Procedure:*

This should be played toward the end of the school year, as it requires precise listening and ordering skills. Give a word of a sentence to four or five children. (In other words, the sentences will be four or five words long.) After giving each child a word of the sentence, repeat the sentence and have others repeat it. The children who have been given a word must now put themselves in the order in which those words were spoken. For example, suppose you gave this sentence: "The dog is wet." The child with *The* must line up first, *dog* is second, and so on. The other children are the judges.

Try this in your spare minutes for a few days, and when parent helpers are around, give the helpers a small group of children with sentences that will include every child in the group. You should write the sentences for the helpers to use.

The children will all be involved, and they will learn to order sequentially much faster.

This process will be difficult for some of the slower children, but with the help of faster learning children, they too will soon be able to order sequentially.

Try the same approach with the order of numerals, without any visual stimulation from cards. Give each child a numeral. Each must be able to remember it and be able to get in order at the proper time for correct sequential ordering. Start with a few numbers, and add gradually.

## Effective Ways to Develop Visual-Motor Perception

### #13. "Card Puzzles"

*Objectives:*

1. To develop visual-motor skills,
2. To enjoy a learning situation.
3. To re-use a product.

*Procedure:*

Save all Christmas, Easter, and Valentine cards for use during the following season. Cut the cards into puzzles and give to the children during parties or during the regular work periods in the month of the holiday. The children can see who can put them together first, or they can see how many of the cards they can put together.

For those children whose visual discrimination is very good, give them two cards of differing patterns and colors. They should then decide on the pieces belonging to each card.

If you know of people in your area who sell Christmas cards from their homes, ask them if you can have their seller's books when the season is over. They are beautiful cards, sturdy and colorful. They also are in a book that can be stored easily until the following year.

#14. "Find the Numerals"

*Objectives:*

1. To develop visual-motor skills.
2. To reinforce correct numeral-writing practice.
3. To enjoy a writing assignment.

*Procedure:*

On a master set, draw objects within which you can place several numerals, but only one different numeral in each object. (See Figure 12-2 for examples of each of the objects and the representative numerals one through nine.)

**Figure 12-2**

With a crayon, the children trace over all the numerals

within each object. Do not have the children find any numerals that are not written upright.

## Exciting Ways to Develop Perceptual Skills Through Relays

Relays are very exciting for all participants, regardless of age. When specific developmental skills are added, kindergarteners are improving in coordination, learning give-and-take, and having a delightful time.

### #15. "Easter Egg Push"

*Objectives for procedures 15-19:*

1. To develop visual-motor skills.
2. To develop tactile skills.
3. To improve cooperation between class members.
4. To have an enjoyable time.

*Procedure:*

During the Easter season, line up the children in two rows behind a marked line. If you have helpers, divide into four groups—two teams with you and two with the helpers.

Using plastic eggs, each child who is first in line starts pushing the egg to a goal line with his nose. Once he arrives at the goal line, he picks up the egg and races back to the second child, who repeats the process, and so on. The team that finishes first is the winner.

The egg may be pushed with the chin, elbow, shoulder, wrist, etc. If the plastic egg is too light and rolls around too much, fill it with candy to make it easier to control.

### #16. "Hit the Cup"

*Procedure:*

Tie a heavy cord across the room, four to six feet high. On the cord, clip paper or Styrofoam cups with clothespins. The children are divided into teams and are standing behind a marked line. Each child throws a sponge ball, button, penny, or other small item at the cups. After each child throws, he should step aside and allow the next to have his turn.

If a cup is hit, the team gets one point. If the item goes into a cup, the team gets five points. A helper should be standing by to help keep score for one team.

The cups should be fairly close together if you play this at the beginning of school. Later, space the cups farther apart. You can also move the children farther from the cups.

### #17. "Paper Plate Throw"

*Procedure:*

Divide the children into two groups. Mark an area around each of the groups. The children must stay within this boundary and must not let the paper plate outside the boundary.

You must give strict rules for this game. The children must sail the paper plate to their opponents, but it must be sailed carefully and not deliberately sailed outside the boundary. If a team does sail carelessly, they are the ones who lose a point rather than the other team.

The object of the game is to sail the plate from one team to the other in order that they can catch it. If it is caught, the team receives a point. If it is done carefully (and you can leave out the point system), the children will gain a lot of pride in being able to catch the plate, and they will develop coordination and cooperation.

If you wish, try one of the toys on the market for this purpose, It is sturdier and probably will be easier to catch. However, the children will have to be especially careful not to throw so that they hit someone.

### #18. "Pitching Pennies"

*Procedure:*

Divide the class into teams. If you have a helper, let her take two teams for the game. The children should line up behind a marked line. Each team has an egg carton, with the top removed, placed a short distance from the starting line. Be sure the carton is stationary. Give each child a penny or play coin. After each child pitches his penny, he should step aside to allow his teammates to pitch. When everyone has had a turn, the pennies should be counted to see which side has won.

### #19. "Straw Carry"

*Procedure:*

With the children divided into teams and lined up behind a line, each child steps up to the line, picks up a straw, and with the straw he sucks up a piece of paper and carries it to a goal line.

Place a handful of straws on a chair or small table beside each team. Place several small pieces of paper beside the straws. As each child steps up, he must wait until the child before him has put his paper in a box at the goal line before he can pick up his straw and paper. He must not touch the paper with his hands. If, at any time, a child touches the paper, he must go back to the beginning and start again. The team who finishes first is the winner.

Bean, corn, small gravel, etc., can be carried in a utensil from one line to another. The children should first carry some in a spoon. Later, you can give them something that will take a little more dexterity with which to carry the items.

Even though the chapters in this book have dealt with subject areas, the skills are all interrelated with the perceptual attributes that you wish all children to attain.

Use the exercises. Change them to fill your needs. Improve them, but above all, enjoy the activities you do with your children!

# INDEX OF ACTIVITIES

# INDEX OF ACTIVITIES*

*Indicates illustrations*